"*Just Spirituality* is a compelling call to a living faith that brings together Christian spirituality and social activism. Mae Cannon uses biographical narratives of Christian leaders to introduce and connect us to spiritual disciplines that anchor our lives as people working for justice. This book is an important read for activists seeking spiritual balance and contemplatives seeking a worldly vocation."

Curtiss Paul DeYoung, professor of reconciliation studies, Bethel University, author, *Living Faith: How Faith Inspires Social Justice*

"This book helps us to develop the kind of deep and pervasive spirituality that can provide motivation and inspiration for activists committed to social justice. Along with her own concrete directives, Mae Cannon taps into the resources of saints both ancient and modern who can nurture those who will to do God's work in the world."

Tony Campolo, Ph.D., professor emeritus, Eastern University

"A book that theologically integrates spirituality and mission is compelling enough. But when it also lifts up faith heroes—both historical and contemporary—who have exemplified this integration, it goes from worth reading to must reading. Mae Cannon's *Just Spirituality* is such a book, as it puts names and faces to faith-inspired activism. As I met these people throughout the book, I kept saying to myself, I want to be like them. And fortunately, Cannon had people like me in mind, as she has provided guidelines to practice the disciplines in a way that releases us for mission. It's all here: theology, biography, missiology and spirituality. Let this book change the way we pray, meditate, worship and study the Scriptures, not just for our edification, but also for the transformation of the world."

F. Albert Tizon, Ph.D., associate professor of holistic ministry, Palmer Theological Seminary of Eastern University, director of Word & Deed Network, Evangelicals for Social Action

"A new generation of advocates and activists of justice must face the harsh threat of burnout if and when their spiritual tanks run on empty. Unless they are replenished in Christ through the Spirit, they will never press on for the long haul. Such lack of endurance would be a major roadblock to the advance of justice in their midst. As a fellow traveler and seasoned guide, Mae Elise Cannon practices what she teaches and wisely instructs her readers on a vast array of spiritual resources available to them. She also points to saints who will energize and direct them along the way. *Just Spirituality* is a timely and important work. It shows those zealous for Jesus' just ways how to keep racing well and stay on the path until they reach their final destination, when Jesus' jubilee justice arrives in its fullness."

Paul Louis Metzger, Ph.D., professor of Christian theology & theology of culture, Multnomah Biblical Seminary/Multnomah University, author, *Consuming Jesus: Beyond Race and Class Divisions in a Consumer Church*

"Mae Cannon reminds us that we, too, are surrounded by a great cloud of witnesses. They call us to a life that is more deeply connected to God and more fully poured out for the broken and bruised world that he loves. There is power and calling in her wise guidance into just spirituality."

John Ortberg, senior pastor, Menlo Park Presbyterian Church, Menlo Park, California

"*Just Spirituality* is a much-needed bridge between doing and being, between justice and spiritual formation, between faith and practice. Cannon's book is rooted in the lived experience of activists such as Mother Teresa, Dietrich Bonhoeffer, Watchman Nee and others who worked to bring the shalom and justice of God into their world. Cannon explores how their inward spiritual practices fueled their outward actions. At a time when people focus on either inner work or outer work, it is lovely to find a book that sees the genius of the both/and."

Adele Calhoun, copastor, Redeemer Community Church, Needham/Wellesley, Massachusetts, author, *Invitations from God* and *Spiritual Disciplines Handbook*

"Biblical justice requires a healthy spirituality. Christian spirituality demands a life of justice. Using powerful and relevant historical and contemporary examples, Mae Cannon offers the possibility of a deeply spiritual faith transforming and shaping our Christian mission. Mae Cannon's *Just Spirituality* is now the essential text that integrates justice and spirituality and empowers evangelicals for justice."

Soong-Chan Rah, author of *The Next Evangelicalism*, Milton B. Engebretson Associate Professor of Church Growth and Evangelism, North Park Theological Seminary

"Jesus' gospel is a call to action. The gospel requires us to right wrongs, to heal the broken places of this world. Mae Cannon is doing just that. Read this book for its rich wisdom that fuels activism like Mae's—the kind of activism needed in our world's toughest places."

Rich Stearns, president, World Vision, author, *The Hole in Our Gospel*

"What a fine and much-needed book! Mae Elise Cannon puts together in interesting and readable fashion what can never be separated—Christian spirituality and the work of justice. Even more effectively, she does it by the use of brilliant biographies. There is no ideology to resist or deny here, just some very real people who went all the way with the gospel."

Richard Rohr, O.F.M., Center for Action and Contemplation, Albuquerque, New Mexico

Just Spirituality

How Faith Practices Fuel Social Action

MAE ELISE CANNON

IVP Books

An imprint of InterVarsity Press
Downers Grove, Illinois

InterVarsity Press
P.O. Box 1400, Downers Grove, IL 60515-1426
World Wide Web: www.ivpress.com
E-mail: email@ivpress.com

InterVarsity Press® is the book-publishing division of InterVarsity Christian Fellowship/USA®, a movement of students and faculty active on campus at hundreds of universities, colleges and schools of nursing in the United States of America, and a member movement of the International Fellowship of Evangelical Students. For information about local and regional activities, write Public Relations Dept., InterVarsity Christian Fellowship/USA, 6400 Schroeder Rd., P.O. Box 7895, Madison, WI 53707-7895, or visit the IVCF website at <www.intervarsity.org>.

All Scripture quotations, unless otherwise indicated, are taken from the Holy Bible, New International Version®. NIV®. Copyright ©1973, 1978, 1984 by International Bible Society. Used by permission of Zondervan Publishing House. All rights reserved.

Contemporary stories are told with the permission of those interviewed.

Design: Cindy Kiple
Interior design: Beth Hagenberg
Images: The photograph of Watchman Nee on the cover (far left) is used by permission of Living Stream Ministry, 2431 W. La Palma Ave., Anaheim, CA 92801. All rights reserved.
   Bishop Tutu: Galuschka ullstein/Glowimages.com
   Dietrich Bonhoeffer: Archiv Gerstenberg ullstein/Glowimages.com
   Mother Teresa: amw ullstein/Glowimages.com
   Athens cityscape: © TMSK/iStockphoto
   Martin Luther King Jr.: © Corbis/agefotostock
   Archbishop Oscar Romero: © Bettmann/Corbis

ISBN 978-0-8308-3775-5

Printed in the United States of America ∞

Library of Congress Cataloging-in-Publication Data
A catalog record for this book is available from the Library of Congress.

P	18	17	16	15	14	13	12	11	10	9	8	7	6	5	4	3	2	1
Y	28	27	26	25	24	23	22	21	20	19	18	17	16	15	14	13

Dedicated with sincere appreciation and gratitude

to my spiritual mentors in Christ:

Brother Romuald, Diane Grant, Gilbert Bilezikian, Greg Jao,

Sister Francis, Sibyl Towner, Tamarin Huelin and Thomas Getman.

They are truly heroes of the faith and caretakers of my soul.

Contents

Introduction

THROUGHOUT THE ENTIRE HISTORY of Christianity, holy women and men of God have shown their inner spiritual lives by active engagement in social justice in defense of the poor and oppressed. Some were sanctified (declared "saints") or beatified (declared "blessed"), according to their traditions.[1] Others, such as Oscar Romero, Dietrich Bonhoeffer and Watchman Nee, were martyred because of their faithfulness in living out God's heart for justice. In every era, Christian leaders have shaped compassion and justice movements around the world.

For iconic spiritual figures such as Mother Teresa and Martin Luther King Jr., one might ask how their Christian faith shaped their mission. How did the condition of their souls influence their ability to lead? What is the relationship between their practice of spiritual disciplines and their effectiveness in shaping movements of social change? Is the cultivation of one's soul a requirement of Christian-oriented justice? In considering these questions, I began to look for resources to shed light on particular Christian disciplines practiced by heroes of the faith.

As a Christian leader and activist, I resonate with the social

justice tradition. I live a fast-paced life. I am more productive when
I am busy, but I wrestle with what it means to operate from a sense
of peace rather than one of frenzy. Spiritual rhythms challenge me.
I work for a Christian international development agency. My work
focuses on responding to global poverty and injustice in the Middle
East. I travel several days every month. I work long hours. I am passionate about my job and consider it a privilege to pour myself into
my passion and calling. As deeply meaningful as I find my life and
ministry, I struggle with what it means to be spiritually centered. I
want my life to be fueled by the power of God and intimate connection to the person of Jesus. I wrestle with the connection between my justice-oriented activism and my desire for intimacy with
the Creator.

One of the strengths of the social justice tradition, according to
Richard Foster, is "constantly calling us to a right ordering of society—right relationships and right living."[2] The tradition of social
activism also has significant weaknesses, however. Foster identifies
one of the greatest risks of the social justice stream as "caring for
social needs without reference to the condition of the heart."[3] This
book seeks to address the core of that concern. Why is the cultivation of one's soul so important? What differentiates the engagement of the body of Christ from the justice-oriented action of
other groups? How might we as Christian leaders and servants
learn from those who have gone before us? What can we do to be
molded, shaped and transformed more into the image of Christ in
our work of compassion and justice?

Just Spirituality responds to these questions by looking at
the examples of seven Christian leaders and their practice of spiritual disciplines. Intended to help readers understand the way spiritual practices deeply form our views of and responses to the world,
this book includes historic examples of Christian leaders who have
inspired powerful movements of compassion and justice around

the world: Mother Teresa (India), Dietrich Bonhoeffer (Germany), Watchman Nee (China), Martin Luther King, Jr. (United States), Fairuz (Lebanon), Desmond Tutu (South Africa) and Oscar Romero (El Salvador). How did the spiritual lives of these leaders influence their concern for the poor, their responses to the oppressed and their activism to overturn unjust systems?

Many books have been written about Martin Luther King Jr., Mother Teresa and other significant Christian leaders of justice. This book is unique because it looks more deeply at the specific spiritual lives and practices of these leaders and how faith practices shaped their advocacy. These leaders became some of the most influential servants of justice the world has ever seen. *Just Spirituality* lends greater understanding of the spiritual rootedness of historic justice movements around the world.

Spirituality is the mechanism by which we come to understand God's work in our souls and the world around us. The spiritual lives of Christians are further fostered by discipline and intentional engagement with God through Jesus Christ. *Just Spirituality* presents the case that the practice of disciplines—such as silence, prayer, study, community, worship, sabbath and submission—provide the fuel by which people are inspired to make a difference in the world. These disciplines are not mutually exclusive, and certainly many, if not all, were practiced simultaneously by the spiritual leaders highlighted in this book. It is helpful to look at the distinct nature of each of these spiritual practices, however, in order to consider how we might apply them to our own lives. This book provides lessons from history as Christians in the twenty-first century seek to integrate spiritual lives with God's call to make disciples of all nations, respond to the needs of the least of these and anticipate the kingdom of heaven.

People often ask me whether there is a difference between Christian service and secular responses to needs in the world. I believe strongly that the Christian faith is of huge import and deeply affects the way individuals and groups respond to needs and injustices. Christians must pay close attention to the development of our souls if we desire to live out God's justice in the world. There is a direct correlation between one's relationship with God and actions of kindness, mercy, compassion and justice. The practice of spiritual disciplines empowers and equips Christians to better engage with society and exercise justice.

In addition to introducing a key figure of justice, such as Mother Teresa and Bishop Tutu, each chapter also includes a contemporary person who practices that discipline in her or his own life and ministry. These individuals represent ordinary people doing amazing things: Sami Awad (Palestine); Wenche Miriam (Norway); Princess Zulu (Zambia); and Alexia Salvatierra, Daniel Hill, Efrem Smith, Larry Martin, Mark Labberton and Gary Burge (United States). Each chapter also includes a section on contemporary *praxis* (reflection paired with action) to explore how we might apply that particular spiritual discipline in our lives today.

The first chapter tells the story of Mother Teresa, a Catholic nun who founded the Missionaries of Charity Sisters in Calcutta, India. Mother Teresa's work and ministry has shaped the world's understanding of God's heart for the poor. What was the source of her strength of character and deep-seated love for suffering people? Mother Teresa had a deeply intimate relationship with Jesus that was fostered by several spiritual practices, most remarkably her commitment to silence. She often said: "Souls of prayer are souls of great silence."[4] During her life as a monastic, Mother Teresa understood how the spiritual discipline of silence changes us, inside and out. As a person becomes more connected to themselves and to God, clarity of purpose emerges out of the silence. The spiritual discipline of silence directly motivates and compels people toward other-oriented service.

The second chapter addresses the spiritual discipline of prayer by looking at the model of German pastor and theologian Dietrich Bonhoeffer. Like Mother Teresa, Bonhoeffer understood the relationship between silence and prayer. He said, "To pray is to be silent and at the same time to cry out, before God and in the presence of His Word."[5] Deeply motivated by the Scriptures, Bonhoeffer led a life of strict discipline and personal piety that included rituals of prayer throughout the day for himself and the seminary students he mentored. Bonhoeffer's commitment to prayer sustained his conviction to live out Christian discipleship regardless of the cost.

Chapter three tells the story of Watchman Nee and his profound influence in leading an evangelistic movement across China during the communist revolution. He felt God's call on his life to be a voice warning and inviting others into relationship with Jesus. Self-educated and deeply committed to the study of God's Word, Watchman Nee became one of the most influential evangelists and church planters in the early twentieth century. Nee's devoted commitment to the spiritual discipline of study of Scripture is a marked example of the power of the gospel to build up the body of Christ.

Chapter four expounds upon the life and ministry of Martin Luther King Jr. Known as the esteemed leader of one of the greatest social justice movements in history, King was also one of the greatest preachers of American Protestantism. The community of Montgomery, Alabama, facilitated the growth and spread of King's ministry and the spiritual giant he would become. Richard Foster claims Christian community is one of the major weapons of fighting the global battle against injustice. In pursuit of what King called "beloved community," King understood the transformational power of God at work through the lives of people around him. As a result of God's power through the community of Montgomery, King became one of the leading voices of proclamation on behalf of God's love and justice in the world.

Worship supersedes culture and tradition as a powerful source of prophetic proclamation about God's heart for justice. Chapter five tells the story of the Lebanese Christian singer Fairuz, whose worship and music has penetrated the divides of nationality and religion and become a unifying force for Arabs around the world. Music has often played a significant part in justice-oriented movements, from the hymns of the civil rights movement in the United States to Fairuz's Easter album about the holy city of Jerusalem. Fairuz's personal piety is a source of strength and centeredness for her strong justice-oriented conviction. Her worship music and Christ-centeredness are beautiful expressions of the spiritual discipline of worship as a call to freedom.

Chapter six addresses the desperate need of Christian social activists to observe the sabbath and include rest in their regular patterns of life. Perhaps the most difficult spiritual discipline for those involved in causes against injustice is that of sabbath rest. Throughout the Bible, writers place an emphasis on the observance of the sabbath as a way to honor God and rest from the toils of one's labor. Desmond Tutu, one of the leading reconcilers involved in ending apartheid in South Africa, is a justice-oriented leader who took to heart the commands of Scripture for rest and the observance of the sabbath. Looking at Bishop Tutu's example, one becomes deeply convicted about the necessity of observing the sabbath to enhance movements of justice.

Absolute submission requires the complete denial of self for the sake of Christ. Chapter seven tells the story of Oscar Romero, a Latin American priest who served as the bishop of the Roman Catholic Church in El Salvador. Bishop Romero, who was deeply committed to the faith and regularly engaged in contemplative practices, reminded the church of the need for submission to the cross of Christ. His leadership directly challenged people in power in El Salvador by criticizing injustice, oppression, assassinations and torture. His example and willingness to devote his life to ending injustice is a profound example of the spiritual discipline of submission. The devotion and spiritual intimacy with God of these seven heroes of justice allowed them to permeate the oppression and suffering surrounding them. *Just Spirituality* leans on the example of these men and women while providing practical tools (ideas for *praxis*) for the reader to engage along the way. A study guide at the end of the book provides further opportunity for reflection. Do not feel obligated to read this book quickly or from one chapter to the next. Rather, read slowly, giving yourself time to reflect on spirituality and faith practices in your own life. You may want to read a chapter each week (or month!), individually or as a group, and practice the discipline discussed during that period of time.

Engagement in spiritual practices leads to Christ-centered action through works of justice such as service, discipleship and reconciliation. At the same time, justice-oriented action also leads back to reflection through spiritual practices such as silence, prayer and study. The correlation between reflection and increased social action is not linear. Justice-oriented spirituality is a cyclical process in which social action leads people closer to God; similarly, spiritual disciplines compel people toward increased engagement in social action. The spiritual practices discussed are recursive disciplines that simultaneously draw people closer to the heart of God through reflection and action.

Each of the practices focuses on an aspect of the spiritual life that helps to put us in a place where God can speak, intervene and transform our hearts and minds. Mother Teresa reminds us that the "silence of the heart is necessary so you can hear God."[6] Prayer and

16

1

the study of Scripture are powerful tools by which we can remain connected with our Creator and understand the world. Lest our pride become a stumbling block, community provides an earthly voice to hold us accountable while offering encouragement and admonishment along the way. The Lord is certainly worthy to be praised in our worship. As we gain a better understanding of God's heart for justice, our worship becomes both more holy and righteous. I pray this book might provide some encouragement for rest and observance of the sabbath as we submit ourselves to the powerful and saving person of Christ Jesus.

1

Mother Teresa

FROM SILENCE TO SERVICE

Silence is at the root of our union
with God and with one another.

MOTHER TERESA[1]

T ODAY I WOKE UP VERY EARLY AT my parents' home in rural southern Maryland. The rest of the house is quiet (which is unusual!), and I am entering into the silence of the morning. The view from my parents' living room overlooks the Patuxent River, one of the largest estuaries of the Chesapeake Bay. The water is rolling gently. The sun is just starting to make its mark on the cornfields across the river. I can see the trees along the shoreline gently blowing in the wind. There are soft sounds of birds in the distance and other outside creatures making noise to greet the day. The sounds are soothing. In the stillness of the morning, my heart enters into silence. As I do so, I am reminded of how much one is able to hear when the mind and heart are stilled.

"If we face God in prayer and silence, God speaks to us."[2] Mother Teresa, minister to the poor in Calcutta, reminds us of God's desire

to meet with us in deep silence, alone with him. Silence fosters
relationship as we are stripped of everything and enter into the
intimate presence of God. Mother Teresa says: "In silence He listens
to us; in silence He speaks to our souls. In silence we are granted
the privilege of listening to His voice. Silence of our eyes. Silence
of our ears. Silence of our mouths. Silence of our minds . . . in the
silence of the heart God will speak."[3]

God desires to speak to all people. Silence provides the opportunity to hear the words that God speaks when we are still, quiet
and listening. At times it may seem that only mystics of the faith or
people called to monasticism embrace the spiritual practice of silence. But professionals, clergy and others specifically called to religious life are not the only ones who should embrace the discipline of quiet. Regardless of one's stage of life or vocation, silence
is a gift waiting to be opened and explored.

MOTHER TERESA: SERVANT TO CALCUTTA
AND THE WORLD

Mother Teresa regularly practiced the spiritual discipline of silence
while being an example to the world of life-giving service. Hoards
of books have been written about the life and ministry of Mother
Teresa. I found few, however, that focus specifically on the connection between her personal relationship with Jesus, developed
through spiritual disciplines, and her actions as a servant with the
poorest of the poor in Calcutta. These questions intrigue me: "How
did Mother Teresa develop her heart and love for the poor? And
where did her strength of character and passion for service come
from?" The answers are found in the actions of her daily life, particularly in her regular devotion to prayer and entering into the
presence of God by practices of the faith, most remarkably silence.
Silence fueled Mother Teresa's social action, which manifested
itself through her overwhelmingly powerful ministry with the poor.

At eighteen years old, Mother Teresa joined the Catholic Loreto order in Ireland and took her name from Thérèse of Lisieux. In 1948, she founded the Missionaries of Charity Sisters in Calcutta, India.[4] When asked about her personal history, Mother Teresa said: "By blood, I am Albanian. By citizenship, an Indian. By faith, I am a Catholic nun. As to my calling, I belong to the world. As to my heart, I belong entirely to the Heart of Jesus."[5]

Through sacrifice and endurance, Mother Teresa reminded Christians and nonbelievers that God is the God of love. She is a profound example of how the love of Christ for all people compels us to respond to the deeply troubling needs of humanity through social action. Professor Mary Poplin tells of her personal discipleship serving alongside the Sisters of Charity for two months: "For Mother Teresa, everything was one person at a time—'one, one, one, one' she would say."[6]

Mother Teresa had a deeply intimate relationship with Jesus that was fostered by silence during her life as a monastic. Her practice of silence created room for prayer and space for her relationship with God to grow. For Mother Teresa, silence was a prerequisite to prayer and the ability to meet with God. Prayer, through the means of silence, took upon itself the form of deep intimacy with God and with Jesus. "And when the time comes and we can't pray it is very simple: if Jesus is in my heart let Him pray, let me allow Him to pray in me, to talk to his Father in the silence of my heart," she would say. "If I cannot speak, He will speak; if I cannot pray, He will pray."[7]

One of Mother Teresa's most recognized prayers came to be known as her "business card": "The fruit of silence is prayer; the fruit of prayer is faith; the fruit of faith is love; the fruit of love is service; the fruit of service is peace."[8] She started to distribute this prayer after it received international recognition, and many view these words as the secret to her success in ministry and care for the poor.[9]

Mother Teresa believed the presence of God transforms souls in silence. "Silence gives us a new outlook on everything," she said; "We need silence to be able to touch souls."[10] She recognized and exemplified the powerful connection between silence and service, regularly teaching of their interconnectedness in her conviction to care for the poor: "I shall keep the silence of the heart with greater care so that in the silence of my heart I hear His words of comfort and from the fullness of my heart I comfort Jesus in the distressing disguise of the poor."[11]

DARK NIGHT OF THE SOUL

In many ways, silence is a pathway to what St. John of the Cross called the "Dark Night of the Soul": a time in which one intimately connects with Christ's death on the cross through personal struggle and internal darkness. Years after Mother Teresa's death, her own inner struggles became a hot topic in global media. For Mother Teresa, prayers in the silence were not without great pain, sorrow and struggle. The world was surprised to learn that Mother Teresa, beloved activist, leader and servant to the poorest of the poor, wrestled with a profound inner darkness during her Christian journey. Mary Poplin writes that this period of darkness occurs when one experiences "deep longing for God"; she believes it is in this dark night of the soul that Mother Teresa found the true love of God.[12]

As Mother Teresa delved into the dark hollowness of internal suffering, she used Mary, the mother of Jesus, as a model in the hope that "God would intervene in His own time and way." Brian Kolodiejchuk, biographer of Mother Teresa, tells of the way she inspired the virtue of silence in the sisters around her: "To envelop in silence God's work within her soul, as Mary had at the Annunciation, was for Mother Teresa an expression of reverence and trust," he writes.[13] In her silence, she maintained a serene disposition while at the same time carrying the pain of Calvary. While she went about her daily responsibilities with joy and vigor, "her radiant smile hid an abyss of pain; it veiled the Calvary within."[14]

For Mother Teresa, silence provided a place within which her internal suffering and darkness could be expressed. Her religious training taught and encouraged "silent suffering in union with Jesus Crucified."[15] Kolodiejchuk describes her quiet suffering as a "sacred silence," which concealed her inner struggles as God continued to outwardly bless her ministry: "She believed that His showering so many graces on her work was His way of disguising her secret!"[16]

IN THE SILENCE, GOD SPEAKS

Intimacy with God undergirded Mother Teresa's ministry with a spirit of love. Prayer and silence provided the means for that intimacy. Mother Teresa described God as "the friend of silence" and believed that in one's quiet and stillness, God would always be present—even if at times he, too, might be silent.[17] She rested her practice in the tradition of contemplatives and ascetics who also met God in the silence of the desert, forest and mountain. Mother Teresa believed silence was a means of stripping away people's distracting thoughts and worldly influences in order to "dwell lovingly in His presence—silent, empty, expectant, and motionless."[18]

Silence was both literal and figurative for Mother Teresa. She believed it was necessary for one's tongue to be silenced, but also for the other senses to experience deprivation as well. One's eyes could not be distracted by seeing things out in the world; one's feet must be still in order to provide an emptiness of noise, movement and action: "For this we need silence of the mind, silence of the heart, silence of the eyes, silence of the hands." This would provide space for one to "listen to God speaking in your heart." She promised her disciples: "If you are hungry to hear the voice of God,' you will hear. To hear, you have to cut out all other things."[19] Silence before God means ridding one's surroundings of "all other things" to make room for God to speak. Silence allows one to open one's heart to hear and discern the whispering voice of God. Mother Teresa saw silence as a means to prayer and prayer as a means to the final destination of "the presence of God."[20]

ONENESS WITH GOD: LOVE ENTERS IN

Jesus was the center of Mother Teresa's life and ministry. She taught that silence is a means of learning and knowing the love of God through the person of Christ. In addition, silence was modeled for her by Jesus. She said, "In the tabernacle Jesus is silent. I can understand the majesty of God, but I cannot understand the humility of God. A little piece of bread! Jesus created the whole world and Jesus, whose Precious Blood washed away my sins, is in the tabernacle . . . This silence in the tabernacle, this perfect silence."[21]

Silence provides a means by which one can talk with Jesus and be intimately connected, made one with Christ. "The more silent we are the closer to Jesus we become and the more we are like Jesus, the more holy we become," Mother Teresa said. "So deepen your union with Him by your prayer life." Mother Teresa believed that without silence there could be "no good prayers."[22] Rather, one experiences intimacy with Christ when the presence of God intermingles with the silence, which creates space for conversation between the soul and its Creator. This intimacy culminates in the form of the Eucharist. The tabernacle was a source of energy for Mother Teresa's extensive and demanding activities, giving her strength to work daily among the poor and the dying. Each day she celebrated mass in the morning and observed the Eucharist in the afternoon. Her love and intimacy with Christ were expressed through her care for the poor.[23]

SILENCE AS A MANIFESTATION OF HUMILITY

Mother Teresa also admonished silence as a means to humility. When directing young women in her order, she challenged them to not only keep silence in their hearts but also to exhibit the spirit of silence in conflict with one another. Silence provides space for self-examination and reflection. If someone criticizes, silence is a way of practicing humility and not responding directly to the insult. Mother Teresa saw this practice of silence as an act of love.

She encouraged that one should not make excuses but rather "keep silence with a humble heart," taking advantage of opportunities to acknowledge truth when others point out fault. In this encouragement of personal reflection, Mother Teresa did not mince words: "Have you heard the voice of God? Is my heart silent? If bitter words, angry words come out of your mouth, then your heart is not full with Jesus. From the fullness of the heart the mouth speaks, and in the silence of the heart God speaks."[24]

Mother Teresa taught that humility, through the acknowledgment of weakness and mistakes and by keeping silence, is a manifestation of Christlikeness. She believed that humility is not possible without silence: "Both humility and prayer grow from an ear, mind, and tongue that have lived in silence with God." In the silence of body, mind and spirit, God speaks and reveals himself. "If you face God in prayer and silence, God will speak to you," she said. "Then you will know that you are nothing. It is only when you realize your nothingness, your emptiness, that God can fill you with Himself."[25]

FINDING CALCUTTA: THE DETERMINATION OF ONE'S GOD-ORDAINED PURPOSE

Silence is a means of hearing God within us and of sensing God's heart for us and God's heart for the world. Mother Teresa believed that every person carries God's love and is called to his or her own unique mission of charity. For Mother Teresa, as God speaks in the silence of the heart, the fruit of love is manifested in service.[26] What greater things has God prepared for each of us? Over the past several decades, followers of Christ have longed individually and collectively for a clear sense of purpose. If the sales numbers of Rick Warren's *The Purpose Driven Life* are any indication, people are desperate to know and better understand God's purpose for their lives.

Mother Teresa acknowledged that every person has a unique call on her or his life. We are each called to be ministers of the gospel, but the specific expression of what that looks like will be unique. Nonetheless, she regularly called the church to action and to taking responsibility for the world's poor through acts of service and love.[27]

What does it mean to hear the call of God upon our lives? How do we intentionally pay attention to the Holy Spirit so that we might be ready to act when called? Mary Poplin asked similar questions during her two-month pilgrimage with Mother Teresa and the Missionaries of Charity. After becoming a Christian, Poplin wrestled with the integration of her faith and her vocation. As she attempted to integrate her experiences in Calcutta with her work as an academic, she remembered the words of Mother Teresa, who told her one day, "God doesn't call everybody to work with the poor like he does us. He calls some people to work with the rich. And he doesn't call everybody to be poor like we are. He calls some people to be rich. . . . But God does call everybody to a Calcutta. You have to find yours."[28]

In *Finding Calcutta: What Mother Teresa Taught Me About Meaningful Work and Service,* Poplin tells how her encounters with Mother Teresa and the Missionaries of Charity provoked a crisis in her own life, a crisis that revealed more clearly her purpose and calling. Poplin writes about some of her conclusions: "In Judeo-Christianity, we will suffer for our purpose, and suffering can be redemptive and instructive. . . . We need to attain the desire of our heart—our purpose."[29] Silence serves as a means of helping us find our God-given purpose.

SILENCE AND CARING FOR THE POOR

Mother Teresa's practice of silence was a source of connection with God that strengthened her love for and ministry with the poor. From the silence, she experienced God's love, which compelled her to bring God's love to the poorest of the poor. She would often tell people: "Jesus is not waiting for you in the tabernacle but in the slums, touching, loving the poor."[30] Mother Teresa experienced Jesus in the slums:

> I never forget once I picked up a child six or seven years old from the street and to see the face of the child—hunger, real hunger. So I gave her bread and she started eating the bread crumb by crumb like this. And I said, "Eat the bread, you are hungry. Eat the bread." And she said, "I'm afraid that when the bread is finished, I will be hungry again." So small, she was afraid of being hungry again. She has already experienced the pain of hunger. . . . And that is the greatest injustice.[31]

Mother Teresa's life's motivation was for men, women and children who had been rejected by society to know the love of Jesus. She believed that large organizations and Christian institutions should address issues of injustice and fix the source of the problem.[32] Her role, and the role of the sisters in her order, was to daily be in contact with those who suffered. She felt called to restore their sense of dignity as human beings who also were children of God. Mother Teresa wrote: "The poor are hungry not only for food, they are hungry to be recognized as human beings.

They are hungry for dignity and to be treated as we are treated. They are hungry for our love."[33] Her gift of love, nurtured in the discipline of silence, brought light and dignity to people who suffered in darkness.

SAMI AWAD: SILENCE, MEDITATION AND NONVIOLENT ACTIVISM

Sami Awad was one of the first people who came to mind as I looked for contemporary examples of Christians who practice silence. Sami, who is the founder and executive director of the Holy Land Trust, grew up in the West Bank of the Palestinian territories. His family lost their home as a result of the Arab-Israeli War in 1948. He describes the injustice he felt from a very early age, "As a young child, I knew and was fully conscious that this is wrong and shouldn't be the way it is."[34] Sami was very influenced by his uncle Mubarak, who showed him that nonviolence was a viable option in responding to injustice. Sami says, "Mubarak taught me how to engage nonviolence from a spiritual and practical perspective in order to pursue the rights, dignity and respect that all people might be treated equally as human." Under his uncle's tutelage, Sami began to join nonviolent protests when he was only twelve years old. When Sami was sixteen, his uncle was deported because of his work in nonviolence. This occurrence was a turning point in Sami's life: "My uncle's deportation created an opening in my life. I decided to commit my life to studying, understanding and engaging what nonviolence is all about." Nonviolence as a way to pursue justice and reconciliation is, for Sami, a source of transformation and healing.

Sami Awad has dedicated his life to pursuing nonviolence as a means of exposing the occupation, human rights violations and injustices occurring in the Holy Land on a daily basis. Sami acknowledges the deep and historic suffering of the Jewish people.

Out of their suffering and the abhorrent losses experienced during the Holocaust, Jews sought safety and security in the historic land of Palestine. Sami believes that even those experiencing oppression are obligated to contribute to the healing of those who are acting against them. True justice is not about freedom for one party and the oppression of another. Sami asserts, "The greatest justice we can offer to Israeli Jews as Palestinians is by creating, through our actions and dialogue, a mechanism for healing and reconciliation from historic wounds."

As a Palestinian Christian, Sami's faith deeply influences his work and commitment to nonviolence. He says, "Even though I grew up in a Christian evangelical family and had a personal experience accepting Christ as my Savior as a young child, it was not until very recently that I was able to fully understand how faith needs to be fully centered in my work and in the activities that I do and the conversations I have." Initially he engaged in nonviolent activism because it was strategic and pragmatic. As his faith became increasingly real, however, he began to ask how he should respond to his circumstances as a follower of Jesus. On a daily basis, he asks himself what his life should look like as a follower of Christ. How does his relationship with Jesus affect his interactions with his family, his community, the staff he oversees and others? Sami describes it this way: "Historically, Jesus hovered around my life. But now, more and more, I am learning to understand and to integrate my faith. Jesus is increasingly at the center of my life and the work that I do."

Sami's leadership at the Holy Land Trust and his commitment to nonviolence is deeply integrated with his personal relationship with Christ and his pursuit of Christian discipleship. As I have gotten to know Sami, I have been impressed with his daily commitment to silence and meditation. He says, "Silence and meditation are very important to me. On a daily basis, I remind myself of the ministry of Jesus and how it began with silence: going to a place for reflection, meditation and personal prayer." Jesus spent forty days and forty nights in the desert before the launch of his earthly ministry. Sami says, "This is meaningful for me as I seek to be a person who follows in the footsteps of Jesus in order to reach a point of awareness, consciousness and personal strength to deal with my own issues and shortcomings." Silence and meditation serve as means of prayer for Sami, and he says he notices a difference in his demeanor and spirit when he does not create the time and space for quiet and solitude.

When Sami first began in nonviolent engagement, he actively pursued it as a means of resistance and strategic organizing in order to end the occupation of the Palestinian territories. Now, having spent several years practicing a period of silence daily, his understanding of nonviolent resistance has changed. No longer does he approach nonviolence simply as a means of resistance; rather, he sees it as a global approach to healing. He believes this methodology can be applied in any community in which there are historic wounds.

Sami is committed to a peaceful future between Israelis and Palestinians—one that acknowledges and preserves the right of Israel for stability and security and the right of Palestinians for freedom and justice. His work and ministry, however, are not limited to the conflict in the Holy Land. Sami cares deeply about people suffering all over the world. In September 2011, he wrote an article entitled "Giving 1 Percent of Jesus to Somalia," which brought attention to the children suffering from famine, for *The Huffington Post*.[35] He called Christians to respond to the cries of those who barely have enough food to survive.

Sami's daily practice of silence and meditation is a source of his care for the world. Whenever he has a challenge or is facing an important decision in his life, Sami sets aside a time of quiet, within which he can clear his mind and make space for God. He first learned this practice from a Jesuit monastery in Switzerland. He has been to the center several times and has increasingly committed to creating space for intentional meditation and silence. The process of emptying allows room for one to better understand and interpret one's thoughts, Sami says; it is about "honoring them [thoughts] and letting them go." He says, "The moment you empty out the space of what you were taught about your identity . . . then you move beyond that space . . . and have the opportunity to make a choice about who you are being called to be." As a result of his regular meditation, Sami believes he has a deeper understanding of Jesus and of the person Jesus has called him to be.

As Sami talked about the daily discipline of practicing silence, I asked him if it was difficult. At first, he says, it was. "At first, my biggest difficulty was my own thinking," he recalls. As he has more regularly entered into the practice, he finds the space refreshing and enlightening. Not only is there great personal benefit in terms of creating space for the soul, Sami says, but he also notices a distinct change in the way he leads. "My ministry is different because of the way I have been able to free myself and be liberated from under the constraints and hassle of daily tensions and operations at work. When I start my day in a space of silence, it creates a completely different environment from which I work. . . . I take this with me for the rest of the day."

The silence helps Sami to embrace not only the practice of nonviolence but the spirit of it. He says, "Nonviolence is not only about physical action or lack of physical altercations. It is also about attitude, behavior and thoughts." Sami's goal is to lovingly speak truth while not violating the sanctity and dignity of the people he is standing up against. His pursuit of nonviolence is an extension of his intimacy with God. Empowered by the model of Christ and the nourishment of his soul through silence, Sami seeks to be a reconciler and advocate on behalf of all people.

Contemporary Praxis

Sami Awad and Mother Teresa both provide significant examples of people whose lives and ministries have been deeply empowered by the practice of silence. Silence provides the quiet time and space to listen to God and to listen to our own souls. Entering into silence creates room for God to do the work of transformation. The spiritual discipline of silence changes us, inside and out. Richard Foster calls attention to this "transforming power of silence."[36] As one becomes more connected to one's self and to God, clarity of purpose emerges out of the silence.

Silence is necessary if one wants to deeply root acts of service and ministry in God's heart for justice. As Mother Teresa exemplifies, the practice of silence directly compels people toward other-oriented service. The Quakers' practice of silence provides further evidence of the strong correlation between the integration of silence and service. Quakers have a long connection to ministries of justice and mercy. For example, they were the only group after the Civil War that asked slaveholders to provide compensation to their slaves for their time in bondage. Foster writes that the outcome of the Quaker practice of silence had social impact far greater than their numbers.[37]

For many involved in movements of advocacy in justice, silence can be a challenging discipline. Adele Calhoun writes of this struggle: "And as the silence settles in and nothing seems to be happening, we often struggle with the feeling that we are wasting our time."[38] Men and women who are unsettled by injustice and brokenness in the world can sometimes experience silence as inactivity. In reality, silence can be the most important practice pursued by people involved in ministry and service.

It can be difficult to settle into silence. The world is full of so much external simulation from cell phones, computers, iPads, Twitter, Facebook and other forms of social media. Calhoun addresses the practical difficulties of creating space for silence: "Silence challenges our cultural addiction to amusement, words, music, advertising, noise, alarms and voices. Silence asks for patience and waiting. And both silence and waiting make us uncomfortable."[39] Silence is an anomaly in a world that is rarely quiet or still. In addition, men and women often have personal obligations that push and pull at any attempts for quiet and centeredness. Parents of small children may particularly struggle to find a few moments of silence! These challenges are real and legitimate, but they should not become barriers to this necessary part of our spiritual journeys.

Some spiritual leaders have the privilege of regularly incorporating silence into their spiritual routines. Most people would find it difficult, in the course of their work routines and family obligations, to carve out a day of silence every week or even once a month! Nonetheless, all followers of Christ would benefit from incorporating this practice into their schedules and rhythm of life. For some, it might mean setting aside a Saturday a month to spend time in the discipline of silence. For others, it may mean asking a friend to come and watch the kids for a few hours during the afternoon so that one can enter into silence without the responsibilities of parenting during that time.

Silence can be found even when there is external noise in the world around us. Much of Mother Teresa's life was spent in large cities with lots of people. A biographer writes that she "learned to be interiorly silent and recollected in the midst of much noise and activity."[40] We can learn to do the same. Several books, including Richard Foster's *Celebration of Discipline* and Ruth Haley Barton's *Invitation to Solitude and Silence*, focus on specific methodologies and practices of entering into silence.[41] Once silence begins, the inner chaos of our souls begins to subside and the presence of God is revealed.

Silence helps facilitate the internal transforming power of God. As we enter into silence, we create space in which God can work. Silence allows us to become better lovers of others as we experience the love of God within us. Richard Foster puts it this way: "Like Jesus, we must go away from people so that we can be truly present when we are with people."[42] Silence develops the spirit of patience within us. It equips us with clarity and purpose as we engage in acts of service and mission within the world.

We can be inspired by the commitment of Mother Teresa and the Missionaries of Charity to "carry out an offensive of love, of prayer, of sacrifice on behalf of the poorest of the poor . . . to conquer the world through love and thus bring to everyone's heart the love of God and the proof that God loves the world."[43] Silence is a gift that allows the love of God to be revealed in us and through us. Mother Teresa exemplifies this truth by her example and her words of wisdom: "Both humility and prayer grow from an ear, mind, and tongue that have lived in silence with God, for in the silence of the heart God speaks."[44]

◆ *Centering and Entering In*

Silence, like meditation, is what Quakers often call *centering*. Richard Foster writes in *Celebration of Discipline,* "It is a time to become still, to enter into the recreating silence, to allow the fragmentation of our minds to become centered."[45] Focusing time, space and attention on being still before God allows us to be quiet, listening for the words of God to our hearts, souls and minds.

Silence greets different people in unique ways. Sometimes, the gift of silence is clearing away the mental clutter that keep us frazzled, distracted and worrying about burdens of daily life. Other times, silence is filled with the deep truth of words that God desires to speak to our hearts. Adele Calhoun writes of silence in her *Spiritual Disciplines Handbook:* "The discipline of silence invites us to leave behind the competing demands of our outer world for time alone with Jesus. Silence offers a way of paying attention to the Spirit of God and what he brings to the surface of our souls." Calhoun reminds us, "Silence is a time to rest in God."[46]

If you are in a room with a wall clock or some other timing device, it is possible that when you quiet down and become still, you will hear the clock ticking. Wherever you are, attempt to find a comfortable place. As your body settles, take deep breaths. Sometimes you might need to take several breaths before you start to relax. Listen to some of the noises around you. Welcome them. It is possible to be surrounded by noise but to enter into quiet inside. As you settle into your surroundings, say a prayer and ask God to speak to you during the silence. Remember to breathe slowly and deeply. Allow your mind to empty of the worries, anxieties and to-do lists running through your brain. Let them go. Give them to God. As your mind empties, consider what the Lord might be saying to you in the space that has been created. Listen. Be still. Breathe. Listen. Sometimes the Lord speaks clearly in the quiet. At other times his voice might be a still, small whisper. At times it may be difficult to discern and feel his presence. Rest in the comfort of knowing he is present and with you in the silence.

◆ *Slowing*

John Ortberg has written extensively and spoken often about the practice of slowing and the need to "ruthlessly eliminate hurry from your life."[47] The purpose of this practice is to place ourselves in a position of waiting, a posture of receiving and an attitude of listening. When we hurry from one thing to another, the chatter of the world around us can inhibit us from hearing the still, small voice of God that sometimes comes in a quiet whisper (1 Kings 19:12). John Ortberg believes hurry has a negative effect on our lives; he says, "Love and hurry are fundamentally incompatible. Love always takes time, and time is one thing hurried people don't have."[48] Ortberg suggests that we can intentionally address our tendency to hurry through practical things such as occasionally choosing to drive in the slow line on the highway and picking out the longest line in a grocery store.

I first heard Ortberg talk about this when I was on staff at Willow Creek Community Church. The fast-paced hustle and bustle of the church and its ministries perfectly fed my intensity, drive and passion to make a difference in the world. Sometimes, just walking through the doors of the church building caused my pulse to accelerate with anticipation at what the day would hold. True confessions: I found myself running through the hallways more than once because I was in such a hurry. I decided that an intentional way to practice the art of "slowing" would be *always* using the hand driers in the restroom after I'd washed my hands. Remember the kind of drying machines on which you push the button and the hot air blows for several minutes? Sometimes it felt like an eternity! Nonetheless, the simple task of taking a few extra deep breaths and attempting to slow down while waiting for the machine to finish its business was good for me! Now, several years later, I am in trouble because most of the machines that dry your hands in bathrooms are now on sensors; once you move your hands, they shut off automatically. For a while I tried to sing a song like *Jesus Loves Me* to practice the art of slowing during my hand-washing ritual. Of course, I found that one can sing a song *very quickly* if in a hurry!

◆ Retreats of Silence

Over the years, I have participated in and led many retreats of silence. I am regularly overwhelmed by how differently each man and woman experiences a retreat. When I begin a retreat, I am able to say with confidence: "I do not know how the Lord will speak to us in the days ahead, but I know that he will be with us in our silence." I have not once been disappointed. Each and every time, the Lord has revealed himself. Sometimes participants in the silence experience a release of grief and sorrow. Other times a young man or woman will have an encounter of the truth of God's love and forgiveness. Sometimes the silence serves to comfort. At other times the silence provides the space for personal conviction. Silence can be scary, because who knows what will be revealed when the soul is quiet and still? The comfort of knowing God is with us in the silence, however, provides courage to enter in.

I went on my first retreat of silence during the Christmas season of 2002. I was invited by a group called Hungry Souls and was led by Sibyl Towner and Karen Mains. I remember being nervous about the silence. Would I get bored? I imagined being in a group of a few dozen women and suddenly needing to shout out loud to break the quiet. I had many questions. But when I arrived at the retreat center, everything was right in place. Towner and Mains gently guided us into the silence. We were given instructions along the way so that even in the quiet, no one was ever alone.

Since that first retreat, I have tried to do two overnight retreats of silence every year: one during Lent and the other during Advent. In addition, I try to practice one day of silence a month as a part of my own spiritual rhythm. Some months I am more successful than others! Nonetheless, I have found this rhythm to be important in creating quiet time and space to be with God. If you are interested in a silent retreat, do some research to find out about nearby retreat centers. Often retreat locations have spiritual directors or guided retreats that can provide a framework and support for your time away with God.

Advent retreats are my favorite. The season of Advent is one of anticipation: of saying, "Come, Lord Jesus, come." The holidays are so busy, full of family obligations, Christmas activities and other demands. What better time to set aside intentional space and quiet in which our hearts can be settled? My prayer, for myself and others, is that we might have quiet time to reflect upon the true purpose of the Advent season. In the quiet, may we better understand the profound truth of Emmanuel—God with us—as we prepare for the celebration of his birth: "Come, Lord Jesus, come."

2

Dietrich Bonhoeffer

FROM PRAYER TO DISCIPLESHIP

O God,
Early in the morning do I cry unto thee.
Help me to pray,
And to think only of thee.
I cannot pray alone.
In me there is darkness,
But with thee there is light.
I am lonely, but thou leavest me not.
I am feeble in heart, but thou leavest me not.
I am restless, but with thee there is peace.
In me there is bitterness, but with thee there is patience;
Thy ways are past understanding, but
Thou knowest the way for me.

DIETRICH BONHOEFFER[1]

IN NOVEMBER 2010, I had the opportunity to visit Egypt for the first time. Conducting research about Christianity in the Middle East and the needs of children in the Arab world for Compassion

International, I arrived in Cairo without significant expectations. I pictured Egypt as the land of the Nile River and the pyramids. I vaguely remembered biblical references to Egypt as the land of the pharaohs and the place of enslavement for the Israelites before their deliverance by Moses. These are not contemporary references, to say the least.

Over the days of my visit, I fell in love with the people and land of Egypt. I was introduced to Christians from Alexandria, Cairo and rural Upper Egypt. I consistently saw the vitality of the church and the activity of faithful believers. I was humbled by the fervency of many Christ-followers. Christians comprise only about 10 percent of the 85 million people residing in Egypt. Of that group, 9 percent are Coptic Orthodox Christians, so Protestant believers comprise 1 percent or less of the entire population. Yet despite the small numbers of Christ-followers in a predominantly Muslim country, the gospel is alive and well in Egypt. I visited a Coptic church in a garbage village near Cairo called Mukkatam, where thousands gather to worship, pray and witness miracles of healing and deliverance. I spent time with a large church near Tahrir "Liberation" Square in downtown Cairo, a church that is committed to responding to the needs of their neighbors.

I also witnessed a faithful movement of prayer that exemplifies Christian commitment at its core. Since 2004, a group of faithful Christians has actively been in prayer for twenty-four hours a day, every day of the week. This House of Prayer has committed prayer warriors who pray for an hour at a time before rotating to someone else. Every Monday the group joins together at a prayer gathering at a local church in Cairo to lift up the country of Egypt before the Lord. For more than seven years, this group had gathered to pray for Egypt's government and a transition that would address the vast disparity between the wealthy few and the millions of Egyptians living in abject poverty. Egypt is a wealthy nation, but more than 40 percent of the population lives in severe poverty. Traditionally in government, military and business, the wealthy elites were recognized for corruption and lack of concern for people living in poverty. When 2011 began, the people of Tunisia in northern Africa had grown increasingly frustrated with the number of highly educated youth who could not find jobs and the extreme poverty of their people. Disgusted by the ruling regime, Tunisians took to the streets in a popular revolution, which ultimately resulted in the ousting of their government leadership. On January 25, 2011, the sleeping giant Egypt followed suit. The Egyptian revolution lasted for a few weeks and mobilized one of the greatest popular uprisings in the history of the world. Millions of Egyptians gathered in Tahrir Square in Cairo. Millions took to the streets in Alexandria, Sinai, Malawi and cities all over Egypt. The people, led by youth, cried out for the toppling of the regime led by Mubarak.

The people of Egypt gathered in solidarity, Muslims and Christians exercising nonviolent activism side by side while demanding changes in the militaristic regime. Christians gathered arm in arm to protect Muslims as they prayed five times throughout the day. And Muslims surrounded and protected Christians as they prayed in Tahrir and throughout Egypt. As the government sought to resist the protest by inciting violence, the Egyptian people did not take up arms. Egyptians protested police brutality, excessive force by the military and corruption in the government. The cross and the crescent, symbolizing solidarity between Christians and Muslims, became signs of the revolution.

The prayer warriors in Cairo and across Egypt experienced the movement of the revolution in large part as a direct response to their prayers. For almost a decade, they had been diligently going before the Lord in prayer, asking for his intervention. These Christians prayed out of the desire for a better future. Compelled by concern for the millions of people living in poverty—from the garbage villages in Cairo to the thousands of residents in small villages in the southern part of Upper Egypt—they prayed. They prayed for change. They prayed out of a deep-seated desire for hope. They prayed that their government might be overturned and that a new future might be possible. At the time of this writing, the future of Egypt remains unclear. Mubarak's regime and many of the former government officials are no longer in power. Parliamentary elections followed suit, a new constitution was drafted and Egyptians elected a new president. The future is not without fear as concerns about how the new leaders might use their power remain. Nonetheless, the faithful prayer warriors of Egypt have seen their prayers for change become a reality. They continue to gather, asking for divine intervention while trusting in God's provision along the way.

DIETRICH BONHOEFFER

The practice of prayer, exemplified by the Egyptian church leading up to the 2011 revolution, was also modeled by German theologian and resistance leader Dietrich Bonhoeffer. Bonhoeffer grew up in Berlin in the early twentieth century. In his early adult years, Bonhoeffer studied theology in Berlin, and in 1930 he spent a year at Union Theological Seminary in New York. As an academic theologian and a devout Christian, he was fascinated by "the struggle of the Negro for equality."[2] As the dawn of the Second World War approached, Bonhoeffer began to ask questions about what it meant to be a follower of Christ in Germany.

With the rise of Hitler, the situation for Jews in Germany grew increasingly hostile, progressing from subtle disdain to overt racism and ultimately to the extermination of more than six million Jews in Nazi concentration camps. Yet in the early 1930s, the nightmare that was about to unfold remained beyond that which anyone could have ever imagined.

THE BARMEN DECLARATION AND
THE CONFESSING CHURCH

As a member of the Christian group known as *Die Bekennende Gemeinde* (the Confessing Church), Bonhoeffer and his counterparts "condemned Nazi doctrine and practice" while drawing people's attention to the "dangers of following an unrighteous leader."[3] The Confessing Church had begun as a result of the Barmen Synod in 1934. Bonhoeffer's work and solid theological contributions significantly supported the confessing church in her struggles. Believing the "mandate of the Church is to proclaim the revelation of God in Jesus Christ," Bonhoeffer joined representatives of the Confessing Church in their formal separation from the German national church, which was loyal to Hitler.[4]

In 1935, Bonhoeffer made the decision to return to Germany after spending two years serving a parish in London. He returned to work with the Confessing Church. He took responsibility for training the ordinands at a seminary in Finkenwalde, near the Baltic Sea.[5] In explaining this decision to Reinhold Niebuhr, he wrote, "I will have no right to participate in the reconstruction of Christian life in Germany after the war if I do not share the trials of this time with my people."[6] Bonhoeffer asserted, in the words of one observer, that "he would rather endure the sufferings of war alongside his compatriots" than remain distant from the struggle.[7]

Bonhoeffer spent two years working with the seminary students at Finkenwalde. He served as their pastor and mentor, training them both in spiritual practice and theological education. Bonhoeffer required students to begin each morning with thirty minutes of silent meditation on a scriptural text.[8] He had high demands for their practice of personal piety and prayer.

Bonhoeffer's book *Life Together* is a gathering of the materials he used after he took charge of the underground seminary. Published in Germany in 1938, the book chronicles aspects of their community life and worship.[9] Bonhoeffer believed deeply rooted theological understanding and praxis were critical components of Christian discipleship. Later, in referring to his christological work in *Christ the Center,* he proclaimed: "Here . . . is an arsenal from which the Confessing Church would draw many of its weapons to defeat the German Christians and thus prevent the poison of Nazism from destroying the Church."[10]

After only two years, in September 1937, the Gestapo closed the doors of the seminary in Finkenwalde, thus ending what Bonhoeffer called their "brief experiment in the religious life."[11] By 1940, Bonhoeffer was no longer legally permitted to speak in public. From that point forward, Bonhoeffer traveled around Germany, teaching and preaching to the underground community, because he was forbidden from teaching, writing and staying in Berlin.[12] During these years, Bonhoeffer made a great theological impact. As the war progressed, Bonhoeffer's influence grew because of his conviction to live out Christian discipleship regardless of the cost.

RESISTANCE

As conditions in Germany worsened, Bonhoeffer had limited opportunities for overt public influence and direct resistance. Bonhoeffer was a pacifist. Nonetheless, he came to believe "it is more righteous to take part in eliminating evil than to stand by passively despite its consequences." Theologically, Bonhoeffer began to wrestle with notions of both Christian discipleship and justice. Bonhoeffer lauded the power of the church in action, what he believed to be true ecclesiology, stating that "those who come to the work of mercy and justice from places outside the church are drawn by a power that the church most eloquently bespeaks."[13]

In 1943, Bonhoeffer chose to join with the *Abwehr,* a group of German military intelligence officers plotting to assassinate Hitler.

This ultimately culminated in his arrest and incarceration in Flossenbürg Prison. Bonhoeffer's role in the plot had been that of a courier and intermediary between the plotters and the British government.[14] He spent the next two years in prison for his participation in the assassination attempt.

THE COST OF DISCIPLESHIP: IMPRISONMENT AND DEATH

During incarceration, Bonhoeffer never ceased to play the role of pastor and spiritual mentor. Each day he prayed a sort of daily examen as a part of his morning and evening prayers. Following his mother's Lutheran tradition, Bonhoeffer made the sign of the cross before his morning and evening prayers when in prison. He wrote of how this helped to "objectify" his experience.[15] In addition to his personal spiritual discipline, he maintained a pastoral and encouraging presence to those around him. During his first Christmas in the prison, he wrote "Prayers for Fellow Prisoners," which began with these words: "O God, early in the morning I cry to you. Help me to pray, and to concentrate my thoughts on you; I cannot do this alone."[16]

In prison, Bonhoeffer was comforted by the reminder of God's presence with us at all times. He reflected regularly on the Psalms, particularly verses such as "The day is thine, the night also is thine" (Ps 74:16 KJV). Similarly, he prayed a breath prayer: "Speak, Lord; for thy servant heareth" (1 Sam 3:9 KJV). These reminders of the omnipresence and omnipotence of God brought him comfort in the midst of fearful circumstances. He acknowledged the power of God at all times, writing: "Even in sleep we are in the hands of God or in the power of evil. Even in sleep God can perform His wonders upon us or evil bring us to destruction."[17]

Bonhoeffer confessed that his heart returned to prayer in a sort of desperation when the bombing campaigns occurred: "The heavy air raids, especially the last one, when the windows of the sick-bay were blown out by the land mine, and bottles and medical supplies fell down from the cupboards and shelves, and I lay on the floor in the darkness with little hope of coming through the attack safely, led me back quite simply to prayer and the Bible."[18] He was encouraged by the declaration of the psalmist, "Call upon me in the day of trouble: I will deliver thee, and thou shalt glorify me" (Ps 50:15 kjv).

As Bonhoeffer's final days approached, he continued to diligently practice daily prayer to stay connected to God. On April 9, 1945, the same day as his death, Bonhoeffer led a prayer service for other prisoners. Only three weeks before the end of the war, Bonhoeffer was hanged on direct orders from Hitler himself.[19]

DISCIPLESHIP TOWARD CHRIST

Many consider Bonhoeffer to be one of the greatest theologians of the twentieth century. Not only did his life and teaching embody devotion to Christ, but he stood firm in his convictions about God's heart for justice. Bonhoeffer critiqued Hitler's co-opting of the German church while also loudly and boldly condemning the Nazi practices of oppression toward Jews. Bonhoeffer's convictions were underpinned by his faith in Christ and his theological ideals.

The power of Bonhoeffer's life and message was his willingness to rest in the person and power of Jesus. He wrote: "When the Bible calls for action it does not refer a man to his own powers but to Jesus Christ Himself. 'Without me ye can do nothing' (John 15:5). This sentence is to be taken in the strictest sense. There is really no action without Jesus Christ."[20]

Christian obligation, for Bonhoeffer, demands a life of obedience and discipleship while manifesting the "moral obligation to love."[21] He called his students to live out this principle in word and practice, teaching them to pray for their enemies, to persevere in times of distress and to maintain their closeness with God through prayer and fellowship.[22]

PIETY IN PRACTICE

Bonhoeffer's theology formed his faith, which in turn compelled him to act in direct response to injustices he observed. Bonhoeffer's teachings, reflections and meditations heavily criticized any form of piety that led to increased "occupation with self."[23] For Bonhoeffer, Christianity demands that one pursue a life of personal discipleship and righteousness, but the purpose is never for the sake of self. Social action may or may not follow depending on one's path of obedience. Piety, for Bonhoeffer, does not start with social action. Pious devotion, however, calls for faithful obedience in discipleship. For Bonhoeffer, faithful discipleship meant returning to Germany and ultimately resulted in his death.[24]

Richard Foster writes of Bonhoeffer's pious obedience in *Streams of Living Water:* "God had so built within Bonhoeffer such ingrained habits of virtue that he had the inner spiritual resources for appropriate action."[25] Bonhoeffer's faith practices fueled his social action. Foster argues that Bonhoeffer's deeply pious spiritual discipline is what enabled him to endure imprisonment and suffering at the hands of the Nazi regime.

Bonhoeffer expressed his personal piety in his reading of Scripture, daily meditation and prayer. These practices influenced his perception and response to external "social and political realities."[26] Throughout his life, Bonhoeffer used the Moravians' daily Bible texts called *Losungen* ("watch words") for his daily devotions. Each day included verses from both the Old and the New Testaments. These texts had a great influence on his life and greatly influenced his decision to return to Germany in 1939.[27] In addition to meditative reading of Scripture, Bonhoeffer's most powerful discipline was prayer. David McI. Gracie writes, "The Bible was the school of prayer for Bonhoeffer, a school in which we learn the language of God, and 'repeating God's words after him, we begin to pray to God.'"[28]

GOD AS THE OBJECT OF CHRISTIAN PRAYER

Bonhoeffer held this firm conviction: "God's name, God's kingdom, God's will, must be the primary object of Christian prayer." He identified prayer as the "antithesis of self-display," in which one would "cease to know himself" and instead know only "God whom they called upon."[29] In this, prayer is seen as an act of humility; an act of focused attention toward God and away from self. For Bonhoeffer, prayer must be "addressed to God alone, and is therefore the perfect example of undemonstrative action." This focus on God served to provide perspective and to remind Christian disciples to not rest in "false confidence in our own prayerful efforts."[30]

PRAYER AS THE WORK OF A CHRISTIAN

For Bonhoeffer, the hidden character of the Christian life is revealed through prayer.[31] Prayer provides space within which one can meet with God. The process of prayer diminishes the self and escalates the Creator. Bonhoeffer described it this way: "In prayer we wait in the power of God for the evil to dissipate and the good to rise up. . . . Through prayer we develop the longing, the yearning to sink down deep into the things of God."[32] Prayer serves as the work of a Christian. It connects us with God and connects us with the action to which he has called us.

Bonhoeffer's power and purpose came from his intimacy with God, which was fostered in prayer. If each day begins with such prayer and intercession, Bonhoeffer declared, "We can go to our day's work with confidence."[33] Prayer served as a resource for Bonhoeffer and equipped him to carry out the work he felt the Lord had laid on his heart. He believed: "Our strength and energy for work increase when we have prayed to God to give us the strength we need for our daily work."[34] Thus, prayer equips us to accomplish the work that needs to be done.

PRAYER AS DISCIPLINE

Bonhoeffer did not believe prayer to be easy. In fact, he stated on more than one occasion that "prayer is by no means an obvious or natural activity."[35] Nonetheless, he practiced and encouraged the exercise of prayer throughout daily life. Bonhoeffer believed that morning prayer determines the order and discipline of the day.[36] In this regard, Bonhoeffer demanded regimented discipline. Regular daily prayer embodies the transformational power of God in the life of a Christian. Bonhoeffer encouraged daily prayer, meditation on the Word of God, and "every kind of bodily discipline and asceticism."[37] In this vein, prayer serves as daily sustenance: food for the body and for the soul. Incremental prayers throughout the day keep followers of Christ on track and intimately connected with the will and direction of God.[38]

CORPORATE PRAYER

Bonhoeffer asserted that, in addition to the daily practice of individual prayer, true Christian community must include the practice of corporate prayer. In *Life Together,* he taught his seminary students that "God's Word, the voice of the Church, and our prayers belong together." Corporate prayer reflects a certain "internal order" of how disciplines are expressed in the context of community. As prayer directs people away from self, Bonhoeffer believed corporate prayer emphasizes and places value on communal responsibility.[39]

THE LORD'S PRAYER

Bonhoeffer believed Christians should model their prayer lives after the Lord's Prayer. He said, "Jesus told his disciples not only *how* to pray, but also *what* to pray. The Lord's Prayer is not merely the pattern prayer, it is the way Christians *must* pray."[40] In addition, the Lord's Prayer includes the acknowledgment of guilt, or confession, as a necessary component of prayer. Confession allows receipt of God's forgiveness and an acknowledgment of one's dependence upon God. The Lord's Prayer reassured Jesus' disciples of their participation in the "kingdom of God" because of their fellowship with Christ.[41] All prayers for Christians depend on the person of Jesus.

The Lord's Prayer gives some of the simplest and strongest eschatological vision for social action. As disciples pray for God's kingdom to come to earth, they are similarly compelled to work toward societal change that will be reflective of the kingdom. As there is no slavery in heaven, Christ's followers seek to abolish it here on earth. As there is no injustice in God's kingdom, advocates are compelled to pursue righteousness and justice on earth. As modeled in the Lord's Prayer, Christ-followers embrace social activism as a way of living out their faith in order for the world to become "as it is in heaven."

LARRY MARTIN: INTERNATIONAL JUSTICE MISSION AND THE POWER OF PRAYER

The type of powerful prayer embraced by Bonhoeffer during the throes of Nazi occupation in World War II may not seem relevant to many people living in the twenty-first century. For most Americans, the fear and uncertainty of warfare is not a daily reality. Nonetheless, violent oppression continues to exist around the world. Prayer continues to function both as a means of fostering relationship with Christ and as a powerful way for Christians to actively engage against global injustice.

International Justice Mission (IJM) is a Christian human rights organization that deeply depends on prayer to support its work and mission around the world. IJM was founded in 1997 in order to end violent oppression and injustice. The purpose of IJM is to "restrain the oppressors who are a source of great harm to the vulnerable."[42] IJM was founded by Gary Haugen, a former lawyer at the U.S. Department of Justice and the United Nations' investigator in charge in the aftermath of the Rwandan genocide. By 2011, IJM had more than three hundred professionals committed to prayer and working actively against global injustice around the globe. Larry Martin is the senior vice president of education at IJM. He speaks of their mission: "We want the world to know God's goodness and we want the church to believe that we can be God's agents of providing justice for the poor."[43] Martin believes IJM, through the support of Christians and churches, can make a difference in addressing global injustice. He says, "We believe we can show up and win individual cases of overt and violent oppression around the world. By winning individual cases, we begin to understand what is broken in the system. Then we are equipped to address systemic and structural injustice."[44] Individual cases present the starting point. The goal is to see communities transformed so that violent oppression such as slavery, sex trafficking and forced prostitution will no longer exist. Martin further explains: "Over the years of our work, we have seen certain communities realize tipping points. . . . Corrupt officials and police begin to see benefits in recalibrating their behavior. Things begin to change slowly until they reach a tipping point. These circumstances are a triumph."

Martin says humility is a necessary component of addressing systemic injustice and oppression. He says, "For one, it is an absurd notion that we can be successful at overcoming injustice."[45] Because of the degree and power of violence and oppression, he sees the work of IJM as similar to that of Moses addressing Pharaoh. There is a sort of absurdity. What power did Moses, the son of a Hebrew slave, have to address the ruling power of Egypt during his day? Humility allows people like Moses to say, "We are desperate!" and then move forward, trusting that God will make a way. With the Egyptian army in pursuit, Moses had the faith to lift his staff and trust that God would part the

Red Sea. IJM founder Gary Haugen describes a similar need for God's intervention: "The nature of IJM's work is just so very difficult that we rarely ever imagined we were actually going to be able to take on violent forces of injustice and prevail on our own power. It creates a sense of desperation. We need God in order to do this; to achieve this objective . . . so we need the God of justice to show up."[46] Haugen and IJM workers around the world seek justice with faith that God will intervene. They trust in God's words to Moses, "I am with you" (Gen 26:24). Larry Martin speaks of IJM's commitment to hard work and excellence while at the same time acknowledging that unless "God goes with us . . . we are sunk."[47] IJM workers see faith practices such as prayer as a way to experience the reality of "God with us" while on the journey.

Martin speaks personally of the necessity of prayer in his own life. As he and others at IJM prepare themselves to do "impossible" work, they receive power from God through intimate connection in personal and corporate prayer.[48] Spiritual disciplines are ways people enter into the process of being transformed by God. Martin emphasizes reliance on spiritual formation because of the difficulty of the work IJM is called to do: "Doing justice is handling power with moral excellence."[49] Sometimes people or groups find themselves stewarding power that they are not equipped to handle. Martin warns that when people find themselves in places of power, there is great potential for that power to be abused. Humility, sought through prayer and transformational practices, is needed so individuals can steward power. Martin emphasizes the pressure of the urgent work IJM conducts. He says, "The more urgent the task, the more likely it can seem that we can only live in that space of action."[50] The need for spiritual disciplines becomes clear; prayer is an absolutely vital component of success in IJM's mission.

IJM staff members spend each year reflecting on a "spiritual grace." During 2011, the topic of reflection was *patience*. Gary Haugen believes IJM must be committed to "doing the work of justice while manifesting the fruits of the Spirit . . . for there is tremendous spiritual peril when someone is trying to do something very difficult."[51] On an individual level, every staff person gets a day off for a personal retreat each year.

In addition to their annual retreats, the IJM staff gathers every day for a time of intercession. All staff members, regardless of position, and visitors are invited to gather—physically, if they are in the same office, or on the phone, if they are living and working elsewhere. They pray together daily as a way of acknowledging their dependence on God's intervention in their work. IJM sees prayer as both the means to receive the "miraculous intervention" and the means to "receive [the] power" of the presence of God. The presence of God provides spiritual grace for individual and corporate character, enabling one to "act rightly" and to pursue justice.[52]

In addition to daily corporate intercession, each staff person at IJM starts the day at their desk with thirty minutes of solitude and silence. The time is set aside for listening and prayer and allows staff members to ready themselves for the day. The organization also takes breaks once a quarter for day-long prayer retreats. Martin finds Bonhoeffer's commitment to prayer an inspiration. Having recently read a biography of Bonhoeffer by Eric Metaxas, Martin couldn't help but feel like IJM's practice and commitment to prayer is similar to the discipline Bonhoeffer established in the underground seminary he led.[53]

In addition to IJM's internal practice of prayer, the organization is committed to mobilizing a movement of prayer on behalf of their work around the world. Through an email list, they sent out weekly requests for prayer to more than fourteen thousand intercessors. They also host a global prayer gathering, where more than one thousand people gather to spend committed time together in prayer.[54] These daily, weekly, quarterly and yearly commitments reflect an organization that takes engagement in individual and corporate prayer very seriously. Seeing prayer and the spiritual disciplines as opportunities to connect and commune with their Creator, IJM trusts in God's intervention and power.

CONTEMPORARY PRAXIS

The lessons learned from IJM's organizational commitment to prayer are important. IJM acknowledges that sources of injustice are powerful forces of evil, which must be fought directly by appealing to God for strength, courage and perseverance through prayer. Prayer is definitely a source of power. It is also a means for individuals and communities to connect intimately to Christ.

Prayer is one of the ways Christian activists differ from secular counterparts engaged in social activism and justice-oriented work. Bonhoeffer believed Christian leaders require more time for quiet and prayer because "of our appointment to a special task."[55] Prayer provides direct access to God the Father. According to Bonhoeffer, Christians "are privileged to know that he [God] knows our needs before we ask him. This is what gives Christian prayer its boundless confidence and its joyous certainty."[56] Prayer provides a source of power and connection to God.

Intercession is a form of prayer that allows the person praying to go before God on behalf of another. One intercedes when one requests intervention, support, encouragement or some other response from God on behalf of an individual or group. Bonhoeffer described intercession this way: "But the disciples must ask, they must seek and knock, and then God will hear them. They have to learn that their anxiety and concern for others must drive them to intercession. The promise Christ gives to their prayer is the doughtiest weapon in their armoury."[57]

Bonhoeffer outlined a progression of intercession that begins with the reading of the Word of God. From there one must "pray everything which the Word teaches us" as the coming day is brought before God to cleanse one's "thoughts and intentions before him." Bonhoeffer continued: "We pray above all to be in full communion with Jesus Christ." We must not forget to pray for our own concerns while expounding upon the breadth of opportunity for intercession for others: "No one who has requested our prayers may be left out." Finally, those who are neglected, without others to pray for them, must also be included. We should also express thankfulness to God for others who "help and strengthen us by their intercessions." At the prayer's close, "we do not want to conclude the quiet time of prayer before we have repeated the Amen with great conviction."[58]

PEACEMAKERS' LITANY

For men and women involved in movements of justice and peace-making, prayer must be the root of power that connects the movement to the direction of God's leading. If the Lord is not at work, a movement is doomed to failure. The following litany, written by pastor Jack Knox, can serve as a prayer for God's direction and guidance in movements of peace. (If the prayer is used in a group, the leader should read each section and the group respond corporately by declaring the words in bold.)

Gracious Lord, we dream of a world free of poverty and oppression, and we yearn for a world free of vengeance and violence. We pray for the peace of Jerusalem. Lord in your mercy, **hear our prayer.**

When our hearts ache for the victims of war and oppression, help us to remember that you healed people simply by touching them . . . and give us faith in our ability to comfort and heal bodies, minds and spirits that have been broken by violence. Lord in your mercy, **hear our prayer.**

When the injustices of this world seem too much for us to handle, help us to remember that you fed five thousand people with only five loaves of bread and two fish . . . and give us hope that what we have to offer will turn out to be enough, too. Lord in your mercy, **hear our prayer.**

When the fear of the power and opinions of others tempts us not to speak up for the least among us, help us to remember you dared to turn over the money-changers' tables . . . and give us the courage to risk following you without counting the cost. Lord in your mercy, **hear our prayer.**

When we feel ourselves fill with anger at those who are violent and oppressive, help us remember that you prayed for those who killed you . . . and give us compassion for our enemies, too. Lord in your mercy, **hear our prayer.**

When we tell ourselves that we have given all we can to bring peace to this world, help us to remember your sacrifice . . . and give us the miracle of losing more of ourselves in serving you and our neighbors. Lord in your mercy, **hear our prayer.**

Walk with us, Lord, as we answer your call to be peacemakers. Increase our compassion, generosity and hospitality for the least of your children. Give us courage, patience, serenity, self-honesty and gentleness of spirit needed in a world filled with turmoil and terror. Lord in your mercy, **hear our prayer. Amen.**[59]

◆ *Praying the Scriptures*

Bonhoeffer regularly prayed the Scriptures, particularly psalms, as a part of his daily devotions. He taught that psalms should be prayed as if they were coming from the person of Christ: "We, too, can pray these psalms through Jesus Christ, from the heart of Jesus Christ."[60] The Scriptures provide direction and clarity for how one might pray. Bonhoeffer often prayed psalms on behalf of the Jews who were being driven out of Germany and who suffered so greatly under Nazi oppression.[61] Valuing this practice so greatly, he wrote a book called *Psalms: The Prayer Book of the Bible* where he provided instructions on how Psalms could be read and prayed. According to Eric Metaxas, author of *Bonhoeffer: Pastor, Martyr, Prophet, Spy:* "In one slim book, Bonhoeffer was claiming that Jesus had given his

imprimatur to the Psalms and to the Old Testament; that Christianity was unavoidably Jewish; that the Old Testament is not superseded by the New Testament,
but is inextricably linked with it; and that Jesus was unavoidably Jewish."[62] In addition to its theological significance, *Psalms: The Prayer Book of the Bible* was also
a strong political statement against Hitler's Nazi Germany.

There are several different ways to pray through the Scriptures. One might
simply read the passage out loud while lifting it up as a prayer to the Lord. Another method is choosing a chapter or passage of Scripture. Read out loud one
sentence or verse, and then prayerfully reflect upon it while using the verse as a
source of direction in the content of your prayers. Continue this reading and response throughout the entire selection, and then close with the Lord's Prayer.

In a group, I sometimes like to preselect several passages. I type them up
and distribute them on small slips of paper. When the group enters into prayer
together, the person holding the Scripture passage reads it out loud. That
person might then respond with extemporaneous prayer in response to the
words of Scripture. All of the people who were given different passages then
follow suit. After everyone has prayed through the verses that were distributed,
someone closes the time of prayer by asking for God's blessing and guidance.

◆ Breath Prayer

A breath prayer is a short verse or phrase that can be repeated over and over
again as a prayer submitted to God. Bonhoeffer prayed breath prayers. For many
activists, life moves at a breakneck pace. Breath prayers slow us down and acknowledge that God is the one in control. Breath prayers can also be a means of
focusing our attention on things that are close to the heart of God such as
justice, mercy, compassion, evangelism and personal righteousness.

Breath prayers might be passages of Scripture or may simply be a thought or
idea that resonates with one's heart. Some possible prayers might include:
"Speak, Lord; your servant is listening," or "Come, Lord Jesus, come." These expressions are short, focused thoughts that draw our attention to God. A breath
prayer can be used to continually return our hearts and minds toward centeredness on God.

When you wake up in the morning, begin your day with a moment of silence. Bonhoeffer believed, "Teaching about Christ begins in silence."[63] Then say out loud the prayer you have chosen. As you go about your day, continually recall the prayer to mind. When you feel distracted or frustrated about something, say your breath prayer out loud to return your thoughts to God. You might keep the same breath prayer for a few days, a week or even longer. Allow your prayers to fuel the actions you feel called to take.

◆ Embodiment

Sometimes entering into prayer by literally engaging your entire physical body can be helpful. Bonhoeffer writes, "The right way to approach God is to stretch out our hands and ask of One who we know has the heart of a Father."[64] My spiritual mentor, Sibyl Towner, taught me a way of using our hands to physically enter into the practice of prayer. As you stretch your hands out, first point your palms down, toward the ground. Keep your hands open. Imagine all of the burdens and challenges in your life flowing out of your open palms. You might even want to verbally name the things you desire to let go of: personal sin or temptations, burdens at work or with family, things troubling your heart. Say a prayer of submission and give those things to the Lord. When you have finished, turn your palms around so they face upward. You are now in a posture of receiving. As you pray, imagine the Lord putting into your hands the things you desire. By the power of the Holy Spirit, ask that you might experience and receive the comfort and love of Jesus. Your hands are ready to receive the light and love of the Savior.

In difficult situations such as a prison, where physical freedom is limited, embodiment prayers can help to break through the oppressive nature of the surroundings. Embodiment prayers are particularly relevant where injustice is present. The act of stamping one's feet can be a metaphorical manifestation of stamping out injustice. The Christian band *Delirious* performs a song called "Did You Feel the Mountains Tremble?" written by Matt Redmond and Martin Smith. It includes the imagery of "dancers who dance upon injustice." Embodiment is one of the ways people can mobilize their bodies to worship and engage in prayer.

One of my favorite personal experiences of a prayer of embodiment happened a few years ago when I was working with some women in the Louisiana Correctional Institute for Women. I was leading a day-long workshop about wholeness in Christ. The topic of the day was how to better love God, ourselves and others. About thirty-five women gathered in the room, and as the day began, we spread out and stood up next to our chairs. I led us through a prayer of embodiment that included our minds, bodies and souls.

We started by holding our arms out, opened wide in a posture of receiving. We prayed together and asked God to reveal God self to us during our time together. We then began to name things that we feared and that brought us anxiety or concern as we entered into the day. We called out injustices that had been done against us and injustices we had committed. I and many of the women verbally proclaimed concerns, fears and sin. After we named some of these, I instructed the women to stamp their feet. As our feet pounded the hard concrete floor, one could almost physically feel the concerns dissipating in the room. Finally, we closed by raising our arms up to heaven. We stretched them as high as we could and proclaimed words of praise and adoration to God. One by one, women shouted out affirmations about the goodness of God. With our hands held high, we worshiped and praised our Creator. Not only did we engage our hearts and minds in prayer, but our physical actions embodied the words being spoken. It proved to be a meaningful and powerful experience.

◆ Daily Examen

The daily examen serves as an evening prayer exercise that invites the Lord's presence into a review of that day's activities and encounters. While the daily examen is relevant for everyone seeking to commune with God, it also serves to propel Christians toward action, not only individually but within our families, communities and societies. A component of the daily examen is seeking how God is calling us to engage in the world. This prayer helps to focus our hearts on God while discerning how God might be calling us to act in response to our own sin and suffering in the world.

Father Thomas Ryan of Washington, D.C., writes and teaches about this practice. He has identified four main steps in the spiritual exercise of examen. The first step is the "act of presence": an acknowledgment of the presence of God with you in that moment.[65] After settling in a comfortable place, take a few deep breaths. When you begin to settle, become aware of God's presence. Say a prayer asking God to reveal his presence to you in that moment.

The second step of the examen is what Father Ryan calls a "petition for light, wisdom and humility." Ask God to reveal himself to you. Pray for his light: to see the world clearly and from God's perspective. Pray for his wisdom: to discern what he shows to you. Pray for humility: to accept and learn from the things the Lord has reveals.

The third phase is an examination of the day "with thanksgiving and sorrow." Review your day in your mind. Begin in the morning and remember the different things that happened and the people you encountered. As you recall the day in your mind, consider which parts of the day resonated with your soul. Where did you feel that you were most yourself and most who God wanted you to be? Where did you see acts that brought you closer to God? Where did you see injustice? How did you respond to these experiences? Review your daily activities in light of how you think Jesus might experience or evaluate them. Consider your day in light of God's love for the world. Perhaps there is something for which you should be grateful and give thanks. Perhaps some of your actions might lead you to repentance and sorrow. As you are led, present your day to the Lord. Pray as your heart leads in light of your reflections.

The final phase of the daily examen is what Father Ryan identifies as "new awareness and help for tomorrow." God is constantly with us. Pray that the Lord might bring an increased awareness of ways you are honoring him and ways you might be molded more into his likeness. Look ahead to the day tomorrow and pray for God's intervention. If you have fears or concerns, lay them before the Lord in prayer. If you are looking forward to some things, give those to God as well. If God is calling you toward action, pray for the courage to proceed wisely and boldly. The Lord will be with you as you review your day. Close your daily examen with the Lord's Prayer.

3

Watchman Nee

As children of God we are already in Christ;
we are one with Him. We don't hope to be; it is already done.

WATCHMAN NEE[1]

WHEN I WAS IN COLLEGE, I attended a small Vineyard church
plant in Hyde Park, a neighborhood on the south side of Chicago.
I learned a lot about worship and the power of God's intervention
through the laying on of hands and being part of a discerning community committed to worship and evangelism.

John Wimber, worship artist and founder of the Vineyard
movement, believed "a central task of evangelism is the bold proclamation of the gospel, a clear and precise presentation of the death,
burial and resurrection of Christ."[2] Wimber also believed that true
evangelism is about more than just the dissemination of information; evangelism exhibits its true power when accompanied by
the manifestation of spiritual gifts. Wimber embraced this idea as
power evangelism: "the explanation of the gospel—the clear proclamation of the finished work of Christ on the cross—comes with a

demonstration of God's power through signs and wonders."[3] Wimber described these signs and wonders as manifestations of the Holy Spirit, often in the form of words of knowledge, healing, prophecy and deliverance. Demonstrations of God's power in these forms overcome resistance to the gospel of Christ.[i]

Watchman Nee, a twentieth-century evangelist in China, would agree with Wimber's profession that conversion must go beyond simple intellectual acknowledgment of the authority of Christ. As Christ dwells within those who have experienced conversion, a source of power is revealed. Nee emphasized the power of the gospel within believing Christians.[4] This power provided a source for evangelism and an invitation for others to join in relationship with Christ and the body of believers.

NEE SHU-TSU (WATCHMAN NEE)

On November 4, 1903, Nee Shu-tsu was born into a third-generation Christian family in Foochow, China. Having been dedicated to the Lord prior to his birth, Shu-tsu sensed the call on his life at an early age.[5] Shu-tsu received an English name during some of his early schooling and was referred to as "Henry Nee." His personal conversion happened when he was seventeen years old, upon which he took the name "Watchman To-sheng," which means "watchman's rattle," because he felt that God was calling him to be a voice inviting people into relationship with Jesus.[6] Nee made the decision that he wanted to honor God by being fully consumed by

---

[i]Christians of different backgrounds and traditions differ strongly in their ideas about whether the spiritual gifts, signs and wonders present among the apostles in the New Testament (particularly the book of Acts) are still active in the world today. An excellent book that wrestles with this question is John White's *When the Spirit Comes with Power: Signs & Wonders Among God's People* (Downers Grove, Ill.: InterVarsity Press, 1988). Regardless of one's opinion in that regard, through the evangelistic efforts of Wimber and his disciples, the Vineyard movement today has grown to include hundreds of thousands of people in more than 1,500 churches worldwide.

him. He took a vow of poverty and gave one-third of his income to the poor. One-third he spent on books, and one-third he spent on his personal needs.[7]

Nee was deeply committed to the study of God's Word. Over time he became one of the most influential evangelists and church planters in the early twentieth century. His passion came from his love and depth of knowledge of the Scriptures.[8] The call on Watchman Nee's life was, in the words of biographer Bob Laurent, to "penetrate all of China with the gospel of Jesus Christ."[9] During his years at Trinity College in Foochow, Nee was known as one who evangelized "everyone he knew." He kept his vow of reading through the entire New Testament at least once a week and was nicknamed "Bible Depot" by his friends.[10]

Nee's life was characterized by both abundant ministry and great challenges. In 1922, there was a revival in the Foochow area where Nee lived and ministered. Led by Nee, groups of sixty to eighty men would gather, organize and set out on evangelistic missions throughout the area. Alongside of these outreaches, twenty-four-hour prayer vigils, typically based in a local church building, were held on behalf of the souls of those living in the community. Nee was committed to evangelism, discipleship and the planting of local churches.[11]

Nee's Western contacts helped his ministry and influence grow beyond the scope of his own country. For a time, Nee experienced the support of the London Group of Brethren, one of the most influential evangelical groups in England at the time. Western ministries were largely influenced by his methods of study and evangelism.

In 1934, Nee married the love of his life, Charity Chang, and experienced direct affronts to his missionary activity from his wife's family, outside sources in England and jealous rivals in China.[12] His ministry life was not without severe criticisms, and he struggled with depression as he wrestled with the question of what it meant to be faithful to the call.

In the midst of his health struggles and depression and the increasing communist threat, Nee remained committed to spreading the gospel throughout numerous provinces in China, work that sometimes even risked his life.[13] Nee's movement came to be known as the "Little Flock" movement and spread all over China. Watchman wrote and issued numerous Bible-centered booklets as discipleship tools for the young churches being planted as a part of his Little Flock movement. By mid-1937, Nee's Little Flock movement was being led by 128 full-time apostles in the field.[14] By 1941, the Little Flock movement was reported to have grown to more than seventy thousand members in seven hundred congregations throughout China under the ministry of 128 full-time apostles.[15]

One of Nee's worst episodes of poor health occurred in the middle of his active ministry. After being diagnosed with tuberculosis and becoming seriously ill, he was told that he only had a few short months to live. While on his deathbed, he wrote four volumes of *The Spiritual Man* and then experienced a remarkable recovery. After 176 days of what seemingly were his last days of life, people gathered and prayed in a three-day vigil on his behalf. At the end of that time, Nee was lying in bed and struggling for breath when these verses came to his mind: "By faith you stand" (2 Cor 1:24); "Walk by faith" (2 Cor 5:7 KJV); and "Everything is possible for one who believes" (Mk 9:23).[16] From that moment on, Nee took those words to heart. He got out of bed and struggled to dress himself. He took a few labored steps while remembering the words, "Walk by faith." He walked down the stairs and entered the room where his friends, family and followers had gathered. He then proclaimed the news of his miraculous healing, which they received with great celebration and praise. By the following Sunday morning worship, Nee was so strengthened in his body and spirit that he preached the Word of God for three hours.[17]

COMMUNISM IN CHINA

In 1942, in order to alleviate financial pressures upon the ministry, Nee joined his brother in Shanghai as a part of the China Biological and Chemical Laboratory. He and many other ministers in the Little Flock movement worked part-time to be able to fund the ministry. Many of his followers criticized this decision, because they believed that Nee had sold out to a corporate enterprise. Ultimately, he was dismissed as the lead minister at the church in Shanghai.[18]

In 1949, Mao Zedong's People's Liberation Army took over China, placing it under communist rule. Mao's goal was to evacuate all foreign missionaries and to absorb the church as a part of the communist state. After Mao's publication of "Christian Manifest for Protestant Churches," believers in China knew that their opportunity for evangelism, publication, open worship and evangelism was limited.[19] Nee had the choice to emigrate to a safe international location or to stay with his people and face persecution in China. He made the fateful decision to stay. On Black Saturday, April 27, 1951, many of the intellectuals in Shanghai were arrested. Wealthy landowners and merchants were arrested, tried and executed while their wealth and land was redistributed among the poor peasants and common laborers.[20]

Nee and many others were willing to suffer for the sake of the church under communist rule. One of the unexpected effects of communist persecution in China has been the growth and strength of the underground church. Persecution, rather than stifling the church's growth, in some ways acted as fuel to the fire.[21] Nonetheless, the church and its leaders suffered greatly. Nee felt betrayed when a member of the Little Flock movement wrote an official accusation against the church and him as its most influential leader. Much of Nee's life was marked by false accusations, jealousy, rumors and other incendiary events that challenged his character and ministry. Time and time again, however, Nee chose not to retaliate. He rested in the words of Solomon: "When the Lord takes pleasure in anyone's way, he causes their enemies to make peace with them" (Prov 16:7).[22]

ARREST, IMPRISONMENT AND DEATH

On April 10, 1952, at the age of fifty, Watchman Nee was arrested by officers of the Department of Public Safety for the charge of being a "lawless capitalist."[23] The indictment served against Nee was 2,296 pages long and included accusations ranging from theft and capitalism to imperialist intrigue and counterrevolutionary activities. During this time, more than two thousand members and church leaders were arrested and incarcerated. Many were never heard or seen again.[24] In 1956, Nee was sentenced to fifteen years of imprisonment for these accusations. The reason for his arrest was his faith in Christ and his overt practice and spreading of Christianity. As a result, Nee was publicly humiliated and defamed. An ongoing media onslaught proclaimed the government's accusations against him. Media outlets claimed that Nee and his followers were a "dishonor to the holy name of the Lord, a blot on the church's reputation, and a corruption of gospel truth."[25] In addition, prayer meetings, Bible studies, church gatherings and any other unauthorized activities were declared illegal and severely enforced.

Nee went to prison to serve out his fifteen-year term. In actuality, Nee spent more than twenty years in prison. Few details are known about Nee's life and suffering during those years. In the United States, the year 1966 marked the throes of the civil rights movement and the work of Martin Luther King Jr. At the same time, halfway around the world, Christian evangelist Watchman Nee was starving and suffering in his fourteenth year of captivity in a 4½-feet-by-9½-feet rat-infested cell in Shanghai, China.[26]

During those years, a few stories of Nee's continuing evangelistic efforts from behind bars became public. Biographer Bob
Laurent writes, "Watchman Nee touched more lives for Christ
from the obscurity of his prison cell than he ever had as a free man.
His imprisonment for the crime of being a Christian caught the
imagination of Western Christendom." Nee's life and ministry was
a great inspiration to the Jesus Movement that swept through the
United States in the 1960s and 1970s.

By 1972, after twenty years of incarceration, Watchman Nee's
health had severely deteriorated, and he succumbed to malnu-
trition and his chronic heart condition. Nee's prison sentence included, per day, eight hours of harsh labor, eight hours of "re-
education" and eight hours of darkness in his cell. It is believed
that his diet was so inadequate that he was forced to supplement
his diet by eating bugs.[27] Watchman Shu-tsu Nee died in prison in
1972, becoming a martyr for the gospel in the midst of communist
China. Nee's devoted commitment to the spiritual discipline of the
study of Scripture is a marked example of the power of the gospel
to build up the body of Christ.

SIGNIFICANCE OF GOD'S WORD

Nee believed wholeheartedly in the inerrancy of Scripture: "We
preach all of God's truth and not just a portion of it. . . . You know
that the Bible is our only standard. We are not afraid to preach
the pure Word of the Bible."[28] He viewed the truth revealed in
Scripture as absolute and a revelatory means to understanding
the will of God. In this regard, Nee believed that theology was not
merely theoretical but provided the substance that fueled
Christian action.[29] When speaking, writing or teaching, Nee
would frequently state, "This is the teaching of the Bible." For
Nee, the Scriptures were fundamental and the principle source
for all truth. Similarly, the Scripture was a source and means of

tapping into the "supernatural power of God."[30]

According to Bob Laurent, Nee was "in love with God's Word." This love was evidenced by his rigid discipline and profound study of the Bible. Nee had more than twenty different methods for studying the Bible, which included a general study of all of the books of the Bible, intense studies of particular books and studies in the original languages of Greek and Hebrew. He had one Bible in which he took "copious notes" and another Bible that he purposely kept note-free so that "he could receive fresh insight every time he took it up." He was known as a man "consumed by God's Word."[31]

Nee believed the Word of God is not simply for study and understanding but should provoke people to action. He believed the Scriptures are a guide for what work is "left to be done."[32] Nee believed that all people are called to be ministers of the Word of God and should therefore know and live out the teachings of the Scriptures.[33] He also believed a sort of transference took place, in which God no longer speaks to the world directly, as he did during the days of the Bible, but rather that today, "He will speak through His ministers."[34]

Nee emphasized that good works are not based on human merit but in dependence upon Christ. God was the source of all good works and positive change in the world. Reading Scripture was the faith practice by which someone could become the most connected to God. His goal was bringing honor and glory to God while drawing others toward relationship with him.

CHRIST AT THE CENTER

At the center of Nee's theological understanding of the world was the person of Jesus. He emphasized Christ's death and resurrection as the focal point of his life and ministry. Christ's death on the cross removed human sin and the punishment of death from the lives of all of those who are "already in Christ" through profession of faith and conversion. For Nee, this conversion experience was at the center of his call to ministry. He desired for people to not only profess Christ but also to live lives worthy of the calling. In his book, *Changed into His Likeness,* Nee wrote about a time in his life when he was wrestling to find meaning. In the darkness of his depression, he declared, "sin is defeating me!"[35] He knew that something was wrong and thus turned to God for help and support. Nee began to reflect upon the verse, "I have been crucified with Christ" (Gal 2:20). For months he read the Scriptures and prayed, asking for God to deliver him. He describes the revelation and freedom he experienced from God's Word: "Then one morning I came in my reading to 1 Corinthians 1:30. 'You are in Christ Jesus,' it said. I looked at it again. 'That you are in Christ Jesus, is God's doing!' It was amazing! Then if Christ died, and that is a certain fact, and if God put me into Him, then I must have died too. All at once I saw. I cannot tell you what a wonderful discovery that was."[36]

Because of his personal encounters with Christ, Nee preached, taught and wrote with the credibility of one who had experienced true conversion. He realized the purposes of God in his life and was willing to bear the cross in order to invite others into relationship with Jesus and into responding to the needs of the poor.

THE LATENT POWER OF THE SOUL

In many of his writings, Nee expressed deep concern with the integration of the spirit, soul and body.[37] Nee believed there was profound power captured in the souls of humans. He asserted in *The Latent Power of the Soul:* "In other words, the living soul, which is the result of the coming together of spirit and body, possesses unthinkable supernatural power."[38] This power provides the source of energy, passion and conviction for people committed to Christ. Nee preached regularly: "My hope for today is that you may be helped to know the source and the operations of the latent power of the soul."[39]

Nee taught about how the sin and fall of humanity trapped the "latent power of the soul" and kept its power in "bondage from freer expression." For Christians, this latent power is released "by God through the Holy Spirit." Satan would seek to blind people's hearts and to substitute a false power for the power of the gospel.[40] Thus, people must be dependent upon the Holy Spirit for discernment and submission. The more people are able to tap into the power of the Spirit, the more external expressions of miracles and "remarkable phenomena" are displayed in their lives.[41]

EVANGELISM AND DISCIPLESHIP

One of Nee's lifetime mottos with regard to evangelism was "witness to at least one person every day."[42] As disciples absorbed the truth of God from the Scriptures, they were compelled to evangelize. He taught his disciples that preaching the gospel was only the beginning of Christian witness. Certainly he believed that "sinners should be saved" and should find reassurance, security and contentment in Christ. But that was not enough: "Every born-again child of God must be taught to take His place in that witnessing people. For God does not deal directly with the nations today, but through the Church which is His Body."[43] Nee emphasized the role believers must play in expanding the church through evangelism. Evangelism was not only for those who felt called to full-time vocational ministry but was an expectation of all who considered themselves followers of Christ.

Nee encouraged his disciples to ask God to break their hearts for the "souls of men."[44] Nee's exhortation of others to evangelize was so great that he encouraged his disciples to move into other cities and geographic areas "even if it meant accepting job offers to other cities where they could make their new homes evangelistic centers."[45] His fervor for evangelism was unparalleled and strategic. Nee's goal was that all of China would hear the good news of Christ. He believed in a "geometric progression" of the good news being spread through his region, China and the world. Despite his fervor, he believed that the result of salvation was to be left in God's hands and might be considered a matter of timing rather than one of ineffective witness.[46] He encouraged people's faithfulness in sharing the good news but believed the outcome should be left to God.

Throughout the Little Flock movement, Nee and his disciples practiced creative methods of evangelism. For example, they created their own "witnessing wardrobes," in which they took plain white shirts and wrote bold Christian messages on them in bright red colors. Soon youth and high school students were proudly wearing their shirts, which boldly proclaimed Christian sayings such as "Jesus Christ is a Living Savior" and "God Loved the World of Sinners."[47] One can only imagine that this would have been a sight to behold in Foochow, China, in the early 1930s.

In his methods of discipleship, Nee was counterrevolutionary in many regards. For example, he used the term "brothers" to be gender inclusive. He called both men and women "brothers" to imply inclusivity and the fact that both males and females were colaborers in the work of the gospel. While addressing different roles for men and women in the home, Nee responded: "And who is to say whether the husband's or the wife's responsibilities are the more important? A strong case could be made for both. But in Christ, there can be no male and female. Neither the man nor the woman has any peculiar position. Why? Because Christ is all and is in all. In the spiritual life there is no way to differentiate between male and female. . . . In Christ there is no disparity."[48]

Nee took this gender egalitarianism to such an extent that at times people had to ask a clarifying question. "Are you referring to male brothers or female brothers?" someone once asked.[49] On the other hand, Nee still often practiced strict conservatism in the local church, with men sitting on one side of the congregation and women sitting on the other.[50] While Nee struggled on earth with physical ailments and depression, he desired to be a man whose life was full of the love of Christ. He committed himself to sharing the love of God with others and sacrificed material wealth and opportunity for the cause of his ministry. He spoke honestly about his own struggles in understanding and receiving the love of God through Jesus. The study of Scripture was the faith practice that most fueled his desire for evangelism and making a difference in the world. Nee believed that study should not be disconnected from action. Rather, one studied the Word of God in order to be transformed into the likeness of Christ and to be equipped with the tools of evangelism. Disciples were responsible to preach the good news of the gospel while also responding to the needs of the poor within their communities and beyond.

MARK LABBERTON: EVANGELISM AND JUSTICE

I was first introduced to Mark Labberton through his book *The Dangerous Act of Worship: Living God's Call to Justice.*[51] At that time he was serving as the senior pastor of First Presbyterian Church in Berkeley, California. First Presbyterian is a large church with significant influence in Berkeley and beyond. Mark was known for his commitment to the Scriptures, his emphasis on evangelism and his commitment to engaging with the needs of people around the world. He is a dynamic preacher and teacher of the Word of God who today serves as the Lloyd Ogilvie associate professor of preaching at Fuller Theological Seminary.

Mark Labberton grew up outside of the church. His father was a rationalist who emphasized science and reason and considered religion the purview of "small-minded" people. His father had the sense that "once someone became a Christian, everything would shrink. Your mind, your social relationships, your ability to use reason, your compassion: everything would become small."[52] Labberton tells about his conversion in light of his father's perspective: "When I started reading the New Testament, it surprised me. Jesus was really saying the same thing as my father." For Labberton, Jesus' teaching set the record straight. His father suggested that religion makes the world small, and Labberton discovered that Jesus presented himself as the counterpoint to small thinking.

Labberton describes it this way: "Jesus made an invitation into the life of the kingdom: a spacious place, a world full of need and possibilities." As he read the Scriptures, he found it difficult to find a character in either the Old or New Testament who did not express some form of doubt in the midst of their faith. For him, this was great news! He says, "As someone looking for evidence of not being corralled, this was astonishing to me." He was shocked to learn that this was what Jesus was all about. He found in the Bible that Jesus created space for imagination. The purposes of God were to "enlarge our hearts and minds for God and for the world and our neighbor."

The framework of Labberton's background largely shaped how he came to faith. He found certain instincts in some Christian discipleship movements to be claustrophobic. Similarly, he soon discovered certain denominations that clearly placed limitations on his understanding of the nature of God. Increasingly, he realized he needed to be in a place where the horizons were "deep and wide and varied" and where he would have room to ask questions, explore and engage. The God that Labberton discovered through study of the Scriptures was so much bigger than the small-minded representations of Christianity to which he had previously been exposed.

Several people influenced Labberton on his journey of faith and vocational discovery. He made lifelong friends in college, peers with big visions and faithful life commitments. He tells of how these individuals had great impact on his personal discipleship and vocational pursuits. As different influences in his life introduced him to the Majority World—people around the globe living in extreme poverty—Labberton's own understanding of the gospel changed and began to include a more holistic picture of God's heart for justice. Friends in college such as Tim Dearborn and Steve Hayner added to this perspective, as did Ugandan Christian leader and now bishop Dr. David Zac Niringiye. Niringiye grew up in a humble African village and is now an assistant bishop of the diocese of Kampala, Uganda. Labberton describes Niringiye as one of the most "globally minded people" and tells of the profound impact Niringiye has had upon his own understanding of God's heart for the world. Gary Haugen, another significant influencer, worked as the head of the United Nations' investigation of the Rwandan genocide and then founded the Christian nonprofit International Justice Mission. Labberton describes these individuals as people of "profound religious and spiritual practice, committed to activism because of their deeper and bigger sense of the world." Their hearts for God and commitment to bringing about change here on earth played a large part in Labberton's spiritual discipleship.

Labberton's perspective that God "had a big vision for the world" largely shaped his understanding of evangelism. Devoid of "evangelical anxiety," he never felt evangelism needed to be perfect "with the words just right." Rather, because of God's righteousness and holiness, "evangelism was much more relaxed: less about making the perfect argument and more about entering into the work God was already doing." Coming from a Reformed theological perspective, Labberton's confidence rests in a God who "knows and sees every person." In addition, conversion includes not merely a simple decision but also a process of discipleship and growth toward Christlikeness.

Labberton's love of the Scriptures was unexpected. He initially began to read the Bible simply because he wanted to have a better understanding of the Christian faith. As he read, however, he was discipled by the words he found in the Scriptures. His presuppositions were replaced by an understanding of the authority of the Scriptures. As his knowledge of the Scriptures grew, he became increasingly fascinated by the things he was learning. Ultimately, he decided to pursue his doctorate in hermeneutics, the study of the interpretation of Scripture, because, he says, "I wanted to understand the reading of the Bible and the different literary critical theories that were having so much sway."

Now, as a professor of preaching at Fuller Seminary, Labberton delves into the Word of God every day. He reads it for personal use, reflection and meditation. He also reads it for imagination, guidance and theological vision, which are at the core of what he believes are the tasks of the preacher and teacher. Labberton encourages people just starting out on the journey of faith to begin with the Gospels, "imagining themselves in the narrative" and entering into the "growing and living conversations with Jesus" present in the Word. Labberton asserts that people read the Scripture best in community. He says, "When we hear the Word of God together, it speaks to us differently." In this way, the Word of God is alive and expansive, with increased revelation when we encounter it in the context of others.

One of the particularly positive influences of Labberton's parents was their very strong social conscience. He was taught about people in the world who lived on the margins. He says, "My parents were classic liberal Democrats, who cared deeply for what was being done to and with people." They instilled in him the impact of society upon people. While his parents saw people's suffering and poverty in light of economic and class terms, "Jesus' engagement was in light of God's kingdom." As he increasingly came to understand the gospel, Labberton recognized a "reality calling people to liberty, wholeness and justice."

As a pastor at First Presbyterian in Berkeley, Labberton had the opportunity to travel the world and fellowship with people "living in the worst circumstances." He committed to internalizing the realities he experienced, and he came to understand the significant limitations and lack of material necessities present in the majority of the world. Labberton uses the pulpit and his writing to share the stories of people he has met around the world, thus speaking to many people who cannot travel to the same degree he has. As he developed meaningful relationships with people who are poor, Labberton gained an increased understanding of the ways the poor suffer politically, socially and economically because of injustice and oppression. In response, Labberton and the congregation in Berkeley began to engage more holistically in the community surrounding Berkeley and in other places.

Labberton believes God provides the grace for men and women to be able to make a difference in the world. Labberton says, "It never ceases to amaze me how much justice work can be done but isn't." Political advocacy serves as one of the means Christians can engage in pursuing justice. Advocacy might include letter-writing campaigns, lobbying members of Congress, and other deliberate choices of engagement. Labberton reminds people, however, that "much advocacy work can be done" outside of the realm of political engagement. He believes every Christian must ask God how he wants them to serve, respond and advocate for justice in the world.

Labberton's understanding of justice is both personal and structural. Christian pursuit of justice must begin in the inner workings of the human heart, but it must not stop there. Complete justice will not be realized until it progresses and penetrates the laws of our communities and the workings of our governments. The theological foundation of the Christian pursuit of justice rests in the verse "Love your neighbor as yourself" (Mt 22:39), but is not limited to simply brotherly or sisterly love. There must be communal dimensions to the pursuit of justice. Justice may begin with individual action, but its manifestations must be "sustained by a community that builds up, encourages and ultimately pursues justice as an act of worship."

Labberton's history and example as a former megachurch pastor and current professor of homiletics may not seem like the story of an ordinary Christian activist committed to justice. Yet his example is an inspiration to many. Having come from a non-Christian home, Labberton's conversion and growth into a leading Christian theologian, writer and preacher is profound. Labberton has come to embrace spiritual practices as a necessary means to understanding the heart of God and fueling social action. He has written about the truths he has learned from the Bible about God's heart for the world in *The Dangerous Act of Worship* and *The Dangerous Act of Loving Your Neighbor*.[53]

CONTEMPORARY PRAXIS

The Word of God is powerful and effective. The diligent and purposeful study of Scripture is an important component of the Christian life. For spiritual leaders like Watchman Nee, the study of Scripture provides pillars for life and ministry. Nee's passion for evangelism and the spreading of the gospel was ignited by his love for the Word of God. Nee reminded his followers that the decision to follow Christ was not enough and that discipleship is a critical component of walking with the Lord. We should remember that, historically, men and women have sometimes used the Scriptures to justify acts of oppression and violence. Thus, Christians must take the interpretation of Scripture seriously, prayerfully seeking wisdom and discernment in our understanding of the Word of God. Study is a critical discipline. As we increasingly become inspired by the Scriptures, Christians are empowered to serve as witnesses and evangelists of the good news of Christ, who came to be the light of the world.

In considering how the spiritual discipline of reading and studying Scripture fuels engagement in society, we can find an example in the Red Letter Christians (RLC). RLC is a group of Christians who have committed to paying extra attention and living out the "red letters" found in the Bible, which refer to the direct words of Jesus that appear in red in many Bibles.

Tony Campolo is a Christian leader and activist who talks frequently about the red letters and what it means to put them into action. When I was thirteen years old, I attended the Christian music festival Creation, held in the Appalachian Mountains. I was mesmerized as Campolo preached about our call to love and serve God and also to respond to the needs of the world's poor. Campolo's message was the first time I heard about how critical it is to live out the words of Jesus in Matthew 25: "Whatever you did for one of the least of these brothers and sisters of mine, you did for me" (Mt 25:40). Other than the Newsboys entering the main field by helicopter, Campolo's message is the one that I remember most.

As followers of Christ, we must take the whole of the gospel seriously: the passages that speak of a call to conversion and also the ones that instruct us to pay attention to the poor, the widows and the oppressed. The goal of Red Letter Christians is simple: to take Jesus seriously by endeavoring to live out his radical, countercultural teachings as set forth in Scripture and especially embracing the lifestyle prescribed in the Sermon on the Mount.[54] Watchman Nee and Mark Labberton are examples of Red Letter Christians: people committed to the study of God's Word and to living it out through evangelism and ministry to the poor. Similarly, we are all called to be evangelists and ministers of the gospel while responding to the needs of people in our immediate circles and beyond.

◆ Resources for Scripture Study

Consider using these resources for Scripture study while paying special attention to the red letters of Jesus' teaching.

How to Read the Bible for All Its Worth

An excellent tool and classic resource often used in hermeneutics courses in seminaries around the U.S. is *How to Read the Bible for All Its Worth: A Guide to Understanding the Bible* by Gordon D. Fee and Douglas Stuart. Written by two biblical scholars who address the different types, or genres, of writing in the Bible, this book walks readers through nonnarrative portions that can be less engaging than the portions full of stories, detailed character plots and action. A great primer for seminary-level study of the Scriptures, *How to Read the Bible* serves two primary purposes according to its authors: first, "to find out what the text originally meant" (exegesis) and second, "to hear that same meaning in the variety of new or different contexts of our own day" (hermeneutics).[55]

Living by the Book

At my former church, many of the small groups decided to work through *Living by the Book: The Art and Science of Reading the Bible* as a part of their weekly study. Encouraged and equipped by Jenny Trees, the church's director of spiritual formation, these small groups reported an overwhelmingly positive experience. The book provides strategies for reading thoughtfully, reading imaginatively and reading telescopically. *Living by the Book* offers things to look for in different passages of Scripture while providing helpful keys to interpretation and application. Some passages to consider in using these study methodologies include: Isaiah 58, Matthew 25 and Luke 4.

◆ Inductive Bible Study Hints

I first learned about inductive Bible studies from InterVarsity leader Greg Jao during my days at the University of Chicago. Inductive studies of Scripture seek to understand what is inherently present in the text. They help the reader understand the central truth of a passage through deeper comprehension. This method is explained in more detail in the book *The Bible Study Handbook: A Comprehensive Guide to an Essential Practice* by Lindsay Olesberg.[56]

The first step is to conduct an overview of the entire book from the Bible. An overview can be done by reading the entire book, skimming it, highlighting and taking notes about the main characters and events and capturing your major impressions or thoughts.[57]

The second step is to dissect the book more closely. Look through the book to find which chapters or passages seem to fit together. How might you understand the main characters, events and geography? You might consider writing out a chart or organizing the different sections with unique titles or labels. What seems to be the main theme? And how does that main idea apply to you personally? You can take notes as you progress.

The third step is to look more closely at a chapter or a section of a chapter. What facts do you observe? Make a list. Take notes about the people, places, situation and atmosphere. What are your major impressions from the passage? Take notes. As you read, what strikes you? Provokes you? More specifically, what does the passage say about God? About you?

The fourth step is to break down the passage even further. I like to do this part with the passage typed out on plain white paper. I often use crayons or colored pencils. Create a title for each paragraph or place where you see a natural separation in the text. What connections do you find between the paragraphs? What meaning might there be between the connections? If you are using crayons, you could use different colors to represent different themes. Some questions you might want to ask include: What is happening in the passage? Is there a central truth that is coming to the surface? What is God trying to teach me through this passage?

Consider using this inductive Bible study method on James 2:14-24. How does this passage speak to social action? What does James say is the connection between actions in society (deeds) and faith? How does this passage speak to questions of justice and right action in society? Spend some time reflecting on the application of the passage in your own life. How might God be asking you to respond? Close your time in prayer, inviting God to speak to you through the passage you have just studied.

◆ Creative Discovery of God's Word

As a creative way to better understand the Word of God, I sometimes read a book of the Bible in tandem with a novel or other piece of Christian fiction about the same topic. This practice does not replace inductive and serious study of the Word, but it can help the Bible to come to life in unexpected ways. Ellen Gunderson Traylor is one of my favorite Christian novelists. Many of her books are out of print, but if one can get a hold of them, they are a treasure! The first time I ever did a parallel study like this was with her book *Ruth: A Love Story*. I enjoyed it so much that I wanted to know which parts had come directly from the Word of God. The second time I read it, I used the Scriptures to determine which parts of the story had come directly from the Bible. The book of Ruth had never been as compelling as when I read it parallel to the creative imagination shared through Traylor's writing.

Francine Rivers's *Lineage of Grace* series addresses the lives of five biblical women in the genealogy of Christ: Tamar, Rahab, Ruth, Bathsheba and Mary. Read one of these novellas in conjunction with the passage that speaks of it in the Bible. What do the stories of these women teach you about God's heart for people in poverty, widows, orphans and outcasts? What did you learn about God's feelings toward injustice and sin? Where did you see God's love manifested to the world? Other Christian novels to consider include Walter Wangerin's *Paul, Jesus* or *The Book of God* and C. S. Lewis's Narnia series.

◆ Reading the Word and Memory Verses

Modern technology has provided wonderful ways for the Word of God to be accessible at our fingertips—literally! Many people have smartphones or devices that allow them to access the Internet and special applications that include different translations of the Bible. Some apps will send you a different passage of Scripture every day for study and reflection. Online, Bible Gateway has a search engine and numerous versions of the Bible to assist in personal study or to help readers find passages quickly and easily. You Version is a website that allows users to set up particular reading plans and then keeps track of progress as days go by. It can be set up to send email reminders, words of encouragement and other tools to help people more regularly read the Scriptures.

The Navigators are well known for their methods and emphasis on memorizing the Word of God. Deuteronomy 6 commands the people of God to keep the Word on their minds and hearts. Memorization is a way of internalizing the Scriptures so that different passages are easier to recall. Memorization allows the verse to become a part of you and to be accessible on the tip of the tongue and close to the heart. Before modern technology, youth would often write passages of Scripture on index cards to help them learn and remember different passages. Today the method of memorization may be different, but the value of keeping the Word of God in our hearts has not diminished.

Passages to consider memorizing about God's heart for mercy and justice include: Deuteronomy 16:20, Psalm 11:7, Psalm 101:1, Proverbs 21:15, Isaiah 1:16, Amos 5:24, Zechariah 7:9, Micah 6:8, Matthew 12:20, Matthew 25:34-36, Luke 4:18-19 and Luke 18:7.

◆ Lectio Divina

One of my favorite spiritual practices, and one that helps the Word of God come to life, is *lectio divina*. *Lectio divina* is Latin for "the divine word" or "divine reading." It is a spiritual exercise that emphasizes the process of holy reading through reflection upon the Word of God. Before you begin, choose a passage from Scripture—typically only a few paragraphs. It can be helpful to choose a passage that tells a story or includes vivid imagery. Perhaps start with the story of the man who was lame at the pool of Bethesda (John 5). This exercise can be done individually or in a group. Choose the verses you are going to read before you begin. Once you have chosen the verses, begin your time of reflection by getting comfortable. Then take deep breaths, creating space for the Word of God, which you are about to receive. Be sure to provide a few minutes of silence and space before beginning. When you are ready, slowly read the passage you have chosen out loud. After you have finished reading, close your eyes and sit for a few minutes in silence. In the silence, think about the words you have just received.

After a few moments, slowly read the passage out loud a second time. This time pay attention to what word or phrase most catches your attention. When you have finished, again sit in silence for a few minutes. Spend the time in silence thinking about the word or phrase that stuck out to you. If you are in a group, quietly go around the circle and if people are comfortable, have them share the word or phrase that caught their attention. After sharing, again reenter into the silence and allow space for God to speak.

After the second reading and silence, read the passage out loud a third time. This time, allow the Word of God to speak directly into your life. Listen for how God might be speaking to you personally. After the reading, provide a few minutes of silence to reflect upon the greater meaning of the passage. Ask yourself: What might God be saying to me through his Word? Is there something he might be calling me to do or to change in my life? What instructions, guidance or encouragement am I hearing from the Lord? If you are in a group, it would be appropriate to share with one another the things you are hearing from God. After sharing, once again enter into the silence. Close your time lifting up prayers on one another's behalf.

Discovering Lectio Divina by James C. Wilhoit and Evan B. Howard is a resource to dive deeper into this faith practice.[58]

4

Martin Luther King Jr.

FROM COMMUNITY TO PROCLAMATION

Let freedom ring from every mountainside—from every
molehill in Mississippi, from Stone Mountain of Georgia,
from Lookout Mountain of Tennessee, yes, and from every hill
and mountain of Alabama. From every mountainside let freedom ring.
When this day finally comes, "The morning stars will sing
together and the sons of God will shout for joy."[1]

MARTIN LUTHER KING JR.

SOME OF THE GREATEST BLESSINGS in my life have come from the transformational power of true Christian community. From the time I was small, significant people have loved me and poured energy, time and attention into my personal development and growth. Of course, this includes my mom and dad, who not only cared for me materially from infancy through adulthood but who also instilled in me a sense of confidence and purpose in the world.

During my college years, two people in particular—Tamarin Huelin and Greg Jao—walked alongside of me during some of the most formative years of my life. Both are devout followers of Christ.

My adolescent angst and wrestling with the world was not a pretty thing to accompany, yet they loved me anyway. They taught me many things! These are two of my companions on this sacred journey. David Benner writes in his book *Sacred Companions:* "Christian spirituality involves *working out our existence* within the context of the Christian faith and community."[2] God's desire for all of us is that we might have such sacred companions: people who will be honest with us when we most need a word of truth, who will offer us comfort and care when the world does not feel safe and who are examples of the love of Jesus.

Community plays a critical part in our transformation and development as individuals and collective bodies. The Holy Spirit orchestrates the transformation of our souls. Nonetheless, the people and community around us play a critical role in that development. Christian psychologists Henry Cloud and John Townsend write of this phenomenon in *How We Grow.* They affirm that transformation occurs when we encounter the face of God through our relationships with one another. Engagement in community functions as a spiritual discipline that should be diligently pursued. In this age, many things pull at our attention. It is easy for families to become self-absorbed in the routines of daily life and to miss out on the rich power of being a part of the larger body of Christ.

I have had the privilege of talking to Dr. Gilbert Bilezikian, New Testament scholar and professor emeritus at Wheaton College, about God's heart and passion for community. Many people give credence to his legacy by holding small groups, Bible studies and other gatherings at the coffee shop that bears his name at Willow Creek Community Church. Humble and self-effacing, Bilezikian, more affectionately known as "Dr. B," does not claim credit for the inspiration behind the birth of Willow Creek, one of the largest and most influential megachurches in the twentieth century. Nonetheless, in a New Testament class in the 1970s, Dr. B's teaching on biblical community inspired young Bill Hybels to plant a church modeling the perfect community found in the Trinity. Dr. B's legacy reminds the church of the vital power of community. He writes in his book *Community 101:* "Watch community take on the powers of hell; subdue the rulers, the authorities, the powers of this dark world, and the spiritual forces of evil in the heavenly realms; and bring them bound and screaming for mercy under the transcendental, heaven-and-earth sovereignty of our Lord Jesus Christ."[3]

Community is powerful, and the desire for community is deeply written across the souls of all human beings. Bilezikian writes about the ways the human soul languishes for the "redemptive restoration of community . . . the only certainty of oneness for here and for eternity."[4] Biblical community, which includes our relationships with God and with one another, fills a hole within in us that needs to be filled. This community serves to transform, bring life, challenge, admonish, provoke, humble, encourage, celebrate and love. Community serves as a model for the Christian life. More than anyone I know, Gilbert Bilezikian has taught, preached and lived what it means to be a part of the community of faith. Preacher and leader Martin Luther King Jr. called this the "beloved community."

◆ Kindred Spirits, Purposeful Friendships and Spiritual Direction

David Benner writes in his book *Sacred Companions,* "The hunger for connection is one of the most fundamental desires of the human heart. . . . We were never intended to make the life pilgrimage alone."[5] All people need to be in deeply committed relationships in which they can be honest about their struggles and triumphs. These types of friendships may manifest themselves differently for men and women, but they are still necessary. Some people may have several people who are "kindred spirits," or deep friends. Others may only have one or two people they relate to with such honesty and intimacy. God desires that all of us, however, be in relationship with one another. Community shapes us and hones us. When we allow others into this deep type of relationship, we enter into the transforming power of the beloved community.

Spiritual direction is a unique kind of community. Benner describes it this way: "Spiritual direction is a one-on-one relationship organized around prayer and conversation directed toward deepening intimacy with God."[6] Many denominations and churches offer people trained in spiritual direction who are willing to walk alongside of you as you seek to hear from God. Sometimes people look for a spiritual director when life is particularly demanding or if they have a specific question they are seeking discernment about. Others engage in spiritual direction as a more regular practice of meeting with God. I meet with my spiritual director once a month. She is a constant reminder to me of the presence of God in my life. As I have shared stories about struggles and challenges, she has grieved alongside of me. As I have had opportunities for celebration and joy, she has also been an amazing gift. It can also be helpful to have several people from diverse backgrounds and experiences playing the role of spiritual advisers or influencers in our lives. It is important that we allow not only people who have similar thoughts and ideas to assist in our spiritual growth and development. It can be wonderfully enlightening to have a few diverse spiritual mentors who can offer accountability, support and encouragement along the way.[7]

Beloved Community

Martin Luther King Jr.'s legacy was shaped largely by his belief in and dependence on the beloved community. He envisioned the body of Christ as God's love for the world made manifest within society. Charles Marsh, author of *The Beloved Community*, writes of King's belief: "The logic of King's dream was the theologically specific: beloved community as the realization of divine love in lived social relation."[8] Community serves as God's hands and feet.

The communal nature of community serves as a type of "shared confessional," which provides a "portrait of the Christian faith as a set of social disciplines shaped by gratitude, forgiveness, and reconciliation."[9] This type of divine community is elusive. Community in the world is far from perfect. Anyone who has stepped foot in a church is well aware of that fact. Yet community is critical. Broken and beautiful, the notion of beloved community provides a picture of what God intended for human relationships. Charles Marsh writes: "The beloved community remains broken and scattered, an eschatological hope, yet precisely a hope that intensifies rather than absolves us from responsibilities in the here and now."[10]

In pursuit of the beloved community, those who claim to follow Christ are compelled to engage in the world around them, to be aware of injustice, to advocate for those without power and to love supernaturally when the world seems to get in the way. Marsh writes: "Therefore, as Christians build beloved communities in, through, and outside the church, they must remain humbled by the camaraderie of unbelievers and non-Christians, grateful for their passion, and inspired (if not intrigued) by their pilgrimages and service, even as Christians continue to proclaim exuberantly the story of Jesus as the source of their own compassion and mercy."[11] This phenomenon played a significant role in King's formation as a minister of the gospel and leader of the people: "But in King's hands, the idea of beloved community was invigorated with theological vitality and moral urgency, so that the prospects of social progress came to look less like an evolutionary development and more like a divine gift: 'God is using Montgomery as his proving ground.'"[12]

MARTIN LUTHER KING JR.

October 2011 marked the opening of the Martin Luther King Jr. Memorial in Washington, D.C. People from all over the world now have the opportunity to honor the legacy of King's pursuit of justice for African Americans, people of color and the marginalized in the United States. Across the United States, countless roads, schools, community centers and other venues have been named in honor of

Dr. Martin Luther King Jr. As the best-known leader of the civil rights movement, King sought to end racial discrimination and economic disparity that existed between whites and African Americans. Undergirded by his faith and desire to see the world made right, he proclaimed a message of hope and freedom for all people.

As I considered the life of Martin Luther King Jr., it became increasingly clear the degree to which divine inspiration fueled his actions and advocacy. King was a man of study and a man of prayer. From a very young age, he began to challenge his father's orthodoxy as a conservative Baptist preacher. Later, however, at Morehouse College, King took a course in Bible and expressed, "I came to see that behind the legends and myths of the Book were many profound truths which one could not escape." Thus, while placing a heavy emphasis on the God found in Scripture, King was delivered from fundamentalism.[13] He experienced a personal sense of freedom when he realized one could study and engage the Scriptures with rigor and intellectual excellence that moved beyond the traditional emphasis in the black church on, in the words of one author, "emotion rather than ideas and volume rather than elocution."[14] King chose to focus on systematic theology during his doctoral studies at Boston University's School of Theology, with the hopes of further delving into the discipline of rigorous study and intellectual commitment. King eventually took his first position as a solo pastor in Montgomery, Alabama. In the years to follow, King was increasingly acknowledged for his contributions and leadership in the Montgomery bus boycott of 1955-56.

According to pastor and American historian Troy Jackson, the community of people surrounding King in Montgomery had a profound influence on his emergence as a national leader. Jackson writes that it was because of the community's influence in Montgomery that "King became the face for the national struggle for civil rights."[15] By 1963, *Time* had named King "Man of the Year" for his efforts to change the world by peaceful means. A year later, he became the youngest ever recipient of the Nobel Peace Prize for his nonviolent activism.[16] King's influence did not come from his belief in nonviolence and his commitment to societal change. Rather, the most powerful impetus for King's movement toward nonviolence and activism was deeply rooted in his faith and further propelled by community. God was the source of his inspiration.

From this historic legacy, King came to be known as one of the greatest preachers of American Protestantism and one of the foremost leaders of justice of all time. As the grandson and son of Southern black preachers, King inherited the ethos of prophetic preaching from the African American historical tradition. When secular Americans acknowledge the historic significance of King's oratory, they tend to identify his talks as "speeches." When King's words from "I Have a Dream" resounded over the National Mall, much more than a speech was being made. Rather, a proclamation of truth and justice reverberated through the thousands gathered there as witnesses. Henry Mitchell, author of *Black Preaching,* writes: "Martin Luther King, Jr. was modern America's greatest activist preacher, not in spite of his warm dialogue with the Black masses, but because of it. The 'I Have a Dream' address was in fact a sermon, which drew dialogue from thousands and moved the civil rights cause forward by giant steps on many fronts."[17] King was not simply a great orator; he was at heart a preacher with a prophetic gift of proclamation, which called people to justice and activism on behalf of the poor, downtrodden, discouraged and oppressed.

MONTGOMERY, ALABAMA:
KING SHAPED BY COMMUNITY

In his book *Becoming King: Martin Luther King, Jr. and the Making of a National Leader,* Troy Jackson asserts King experienced a life-changing transformation during his time in community in Montgomery, Alabama. He arrived prepared to pastor Dexter Avenue Baptist Church, but by the time he left to return to Atlanta, "his faith had moved from an intellectual theory to a heartfelt belief. No longer was King's call to ministry only understood as a way to contribute to society. Now ministry was about leading a community to trust in the power, justice, and righteousness of God even when evil seemed to triumph."[18] Charles Marsh concurs that King was transformed by the community in Montgomery: "In Montgomery, Martin Luther King Jr. came to a new understanding of redemptive social relation: the beloved community."[19]

The determination and courage of the men and women of Montgomery not only launched the bus boycott movement in 1955. Their sacrifice and investment in overturning the unjust system of segregation was, in many ways, the spark that launched the civil rights movement. King was greatly influenced by the leadership and resolute conviction of others to directly engage in nonviolent activism to overturn discriminatory laws and practices. This context served as an incubator for King's formation as an activist preacher and leader. Jackson confirms: "Not only did a handful of courageous men and women in Montgomery spearhead a protest movement; they also nurtured, influenced, and helped launch King's public ministry."[20] King would not have been who he came to be if it were not for the formational power of his community experiences in Montgomery, Alabama.

King himself acknowledged the significant role others had played in shaping his call and ministry. He once preached: "Help me, O God, to see that I'm just a symbol of a movement. . . . Help me to realize that I'm where I am because of the forces of history and because of the fifty thousand Negroes of Alabama who will never get their names in the papers and in the headline."[21] He noted, "a boycott would have taken place in Montgomery, Alabama, if I had never come to Alabama."[22] The foot soldiers of the movement were mobilized before King even arrived on the scene. This is not to minimize his significance but to acknowledge the transformational power the community of Montgomery had on his life. Jackson rightly asserts: "King took the lessons of Montgomery with him, as their courage, activism, and sacrifice prepared him for the many battles that awaited him. In the crucible of Montgomery, Martin Luther King Jr. was becoming King the civil rights leader."[23]

INFLUENCE THROUGH NONVIOLENT ACTIVISM

King's embrace of nonviolent activism was one of his greatest contributions in the pursuit of justice for people of color in the United States. As King learned about Gandhi's use of nonviolence and its effectiveness in India, he sought to apply similar principles in the American battle against segregation and injustice. King's preaching and rhetoric was a means to publicly proclaim the truth of nonviolent resistance in the spirit of love. Jackson writes about the way King's sermons reached people of all walks of life. With King's increased visibility, he and his family became targets of violent attacks, including ones with bricks, knives and dynamite. Despite these challenges, "King maintained hope in the prevailing power of God when it is unleashed through the love-infused strategy of nonviolence."[24] The method of nonviolent activism was deeply ingrained in King's notions of beloved community. Values such as "tolerance, reason, humanity, generosity, and justice" functioned as a part of the nature of the beloved community.[25]

THE SOURCE OF KING'S INFLUENCE

King attributed his strength and influence to his faith and relationship with God. In writing about King's connection with God, Lewis Baldwin, the author of *Never to Leave Us Alone: The Prayer Life of Martin Luther King, Jr.*, writes: "King combined a deep personal piety with intellectual ability and a profound social vision."[26] In Montgomery, King's piety was expressed through his role as pastor of Dexter Avenue Baptist Church, in his private connection with God through prayer and in his commitment to community action.

By January 27, 1956, the situation in Montgomery had continued to escalate. King received a death threat on his home telephone. This was not the first time he had received threats against his and his family's lives. But this particular experience was a turning point. King described his emotional state as he sat down at the kitchen table with a cup of coffee; "I was ready to give up," he reflected.[27] Yet, somehow, he found strength in the spiritual intimacy he experienced with God. King later illustrated the source of his power and the words he heard from God: "But Lord, I must confess that I'm weak now. I'm faltering. I'm losing my courage. . . . And it seemed at that moment that I could hear an inner voice saying to me, 'Martin Luther, stand up for righteousness. Stand up for justice. Stand up for truth. And lo I will be with you, even until the end of the world.' . . . I heard the voice of Jesus saying still to fight on. He promised to never leave me, never to leave me alone. No never alone. No never alone."[28]

King realized that he was not alone in his struggle. He also realized that his own strength would not be enough to win the battle ahead. Instead, the magnitude of the task that lay before him required an ultimate dependence on God. This dependence, further fostered by community, was the source of power for King.

PROCLAMATION OF JUSTICE

Participation in the beloved community served as a faith practice for King in his journey as an advocate of justice. God's presence manifested itself in these encounters and informed King's speaking and engagement with society. His oratorical ability and gifted proclamation served as an invitation for others to join the struggle. King invited others into meaningful community. King proclaimed a vision of the kingdom of God on earth, a picture of the way things should be when all people have access to opportunity within a just society. The purpose of proclamation is not only to outwardly remember the promise of Scripture and that the kingdom of God will one day be fully present; the purpose of proclamation is also to publicly expose the horrors of injustice that impede the work of God in our midst. Martin Luther King Jr.'s writing and preaching contain both of these characteristics of calling forth God's kingdom while naming the realities of earthly injustice. In this regard, King came to be identified as the "voice of the movement."[29] In 1990, Henry Mitchell wrote of King's legacy as a part of the historic tradition of black proclamation's dependence on help from God and the belief that "their gospel of God's 'somehow' told our ancestors that slavery would end. It told marchers that segregation would die, and it is still telling Blacks in South Africa that the day of justice is inevitable."[30]

King's oratory was so powerful it served as a tool of advocacy. He spoke into existence the inspiration people needed to be mobilized toward the common goal of justice. While King called the community into action, he was also shaped by the community around him. Historian and King scholar Clayborne Carson writes of this power: "The Montgomery bus boycott would have happened without King, but King's oratory helped to ensure that the boycott became one of those exceptional local movements for justice that would send ripples of inspiration to oppressed people everywhere."[31]

Martin Luther King Jr. was assassinated before I was born. I never had the privilege of hearing him preach when he was alive. I did, however, hear his mentor, Gardner C. Taylor, preach at Saint Sabina Catholic Church in Chicago. Taylor was formerly the pastor of Concord Baptist Church of Christ in Brooklyn. He was a leading voice during the civil rights movement. His preaching and oratorical style had a great influence on King. Many claim Taylor to be the most acclaimed preacher of our time. For as long as I live, I will remember Taylor stepping out to walk across the stage and stand at the pulpit. He is not a large man. He was already close to ninety years old when I heard him preach, and two men needed to accompany him to offer support as he walked toward the pulpit. He was wearing a dark black suit and a bright red tie. As he entered, I was struck by both his frailty and his longevity.

But when Gardner Taylor opened his mouth to proclaim the Word of God, a much younger man stood at the altar. His size seemed to grow tenfold. It was as if the heavens opened and the Word of God came down through the proclamation of this small elderly man standing at the pulpit. The power and conviction of his words had me sitting on the edge of my seat. My adrenaline began to rush as I listened to his compelling message of faith and action. Dr. Taylor proclaimed the Word of God powerfully. His voice was a mobilizing force to action and engagement for the sake of love, mercy and justice.

At the end of the service, all of the ministers were called forward. Taylor laid his hands upon each of us as he blessed us to go and be change agents in the world. I left with a strong conviction that proclamation is a powerful tool to compel others into action. Through that blessing I was also invited into community with Gardner Taylor; my ministry became a small piece of the legacy he will leave behind.

PROCLAMATION AND PROPHECY

King's legacy of proclamation also included the important element of prophecy. King rooted his vision for justice and equality in Scripture and served as a prophetic voice that moved others toward a more holistic picture of society. Richard Lischer wrote in *The Preacher King* about this aspect of King: "In his prophetic ministry, King gave names to what he saw: sin, racism, genocide, doom, cowardice, expediency, idolatry of nation, militarism, religious hypocrisy."[32] King offered an alternative vision of inclusiveness while also admonishing others to heed the scriptural mandates to care for the poor.

King's own transformational development was not only shaped by the community around him; his preaching and leadership also called the community to a different way of living. King was not always appreciated for his prophetic utterances and, in fact, suffered great criticisms for his desire to see society change.

PROCLAMATION FOR CHANGE

King's use of oratory was not only for the personal edification of those listening. He preached with the purpose of provoking change. Baldwin writes of the way King integrated prayer with proclamation for a distinct purpose: "The sermon was an exercise in futility if its impact remained confined within the consecrated walls of the church or if it failed to move both himself and his hearers to positive self- and societal transformation."[33] King's message emphasized the importance of integrating proclamation and practice. He criticized the white church in the South for lacking this integration. Similarly, Charles Marsh highlights the "bifurcation between proclamation and practice" for many white Protestants in the South during the civil rights movement: people who could simultaneously take to heart an evangelical sermon about reconciliation in Paul's letter to the Corinthians on Sunday morning while wholeheartedly denying a gospel message that "requires brotherhood with black people."[34] King's prophetic message had power because he was willing to directly engage and act according to his beliefs. There are many examples of his willingness to take action for the cause. King marched alongside the foot soldiers of the movement. He spent time in jail in Birmingham, Alabama, to help serve the movement there. Ultimately, King became a martyr for the cause of justice when he was assassinated on April 4, 1968, in Memphis, Tennessee.

GARY BURGE: ACADEMIC AND ACTIVIST FOR PEACE

In 2009, I participated in a spiritual pilgrimage to the Holy Land. The intention was that Gilbert Bilezikian would be the guide and spiritual leader. About two weeks before our departure, however, some unexpected health concerns arose that made it impossible for him to travel. Thus, with my divinity degree only a few years old, I delved into preparation to be the leader of a spiritual pilgrimage to a land I had never seen. I was excited to walk in the land where Jesus walked, but I had no idea what was in store for me and our group when we stepped foot in the Holy Land. At the time I was the executive pastor of a church in Northern California; nine congregation members joined me on the trip. Every participant had been asked to read two books: *Blood Brothers* by Bishop Elias Chacour and *Whose Land? Whose Promise?* by Gary Burge. The other nine members of the group were diligent. I was not. I was in a panic, desperately trying to review my seminary courses on biblical geography, the Prophets, wisdom literature and the entire New Testament. I didn't have time to read either of the books for our group.

Our two weeks in the Holy Land made the Scriptures come alive in ways I never thought possible. As our group and other pilgrims were introduced to the holy sites and places throughout the Bible, the stories from Scripture took on a life of their own. We could picture where Jesus gave the Sermon on the Mount, we tasted fish from the Sea of Galilee and some in our group testified to their salvation by getting baptized in the Jordan River. The spiritual significance of that journey cannot be exaggerated.

A second and unforeseen consequence of our visit was that we were introduced to the deep divisions and astounding pain resulting from the Israeli-Palestinian conflict. After two weeks of being introduced to Jews, Muslims and Christians in both Israel and Palestine, I had far more questions than answers. After our pilgrimage was over, we had a few days to travel to Petra, which was several hours by car from Amman. On that road trip along the King's Highway, I began to read Gary Burge's book. I learned about some of the history of the land and people of Israel and Palestine. I was introduced to Palestinian Christians who love Jesus and desire to be recognized and included in the global Christian community. Burge's book clarified for me some of the things I had been introduced to during my visit. Three hours on the King's Highway on the edge of the Arabian Desert in Jordan is enough to give anyone a second calling. God began the process of transforming my heart to desire peace and security for the people of Israel while also seeking justice on behalf of the Palestinians. I am thankful I had Burge's book to keep me company on the journey.

In March 2010, I had my first opportunity to meet Gary in Bethlehem at a conference called "Christ at the Checkpoint." He was giving a lecture about the historical Jesus and a theology of the land in order to provide perspective for a better understanding of the struggle between Israel and Palestine. I am amazed how this professor of New Testament from Wheaton College, which many consider the bastion of evangelicalism, commits himself to teaching about justice in the occupied Palestinian territories. Over the past few decades, Burge has been actively involved in the Middle East and has deeply invested in Arabic-speaking churches in the Palestinian territories, Syria, Iraq and other countries. When I asked him what interests him and compels him to be involved in the Middle East, he responded by identifying two unique character-

istics: the Palestinian encounter with Israeli occupation and what
it means for Christians living as a minority in Muslim countries
throughout the Arab world. Burge proclaims his commitment to
both peace and justice for Israel and Palestine through his teaching
and writing.

Gary Burge is an example of someone who integrates his personal faith and spiritual practice in the pursuit of justice. He believes this engagement with issues of justice occurs when people
have a "second conversion experience."[35] He says: "I am not sure
that a lot of people will pick up a justice issue because they read a
lot. Justice won't just 'dawn' on someone one day. They will have to
have an encounter and to rearrange their priorities." Burge asserts,
"No one is passionate about a justice issue unless they have been
converted." Throughout history, this seems to be the case. Individuals and justice leaders have allowed God to penetrate their
hearts in a supernatural way, giving them a heart for the disposed,
the poor and the neglected.

Bob Pierce, founder of World Vision, is famous for his words:
"Let my heart be broken by the things that break the heart of God."
When we are willing to create community with our neighbors, we
see their pain, loss and suffering in a unique way. We are converted to their cause for the sake of love and for the sake of justice.
Mother Teresa was converted by the lepers of Calcutta. Martin
Luther King Jr. was converted by the mothers, teachers and domestic workers who walked for miles during the Montgomery
bus boycott. Watchman Nee was converted by the lost souls of
his brothers and sisters across China. Bonhoeffer was converted
by the death and destruction of the Jews and other minorities at
the hands of the Nazi regime. Gary Burge was converted when he
came face to face with the deep discord between the people of
Israel and their neighboring Palestinian community. These types
of conversion experiences only happen when we bump directly

into each other in the context of community.

Community is necessary for this type of conversion and transformation. Burge offers valuable insight about the ways people become engaged in issues of justice. For Burge, "Spiritual formation is the process by which we become mature into the likeness of Christ." In describing this conversion toward Christlikeness, he asserts there must be a two-way encounter: first with God and also with the world. One may encounter God through Christian community, reading the Scriptures and other provocations of the soul. This encounter with God doesn't extend beyond individualistic pursuit of righteousness, however, unless a person also has a direct encounter with the world. Burge asserts, "One has to know what the Scriptures say. . . . It is necessary to develop a theology of God in his relationship with the world." Reading Scripture at the same time as one reads the "book of history" allows one to discover what "God's mind might be in the midst of those events." Prophets from the Old Testament certainly understood global politics of their day. Christians must also be reminded of the prophetic side of Christ.

In addition to his call toward personal righteousness, Jesus was also very much engaged in the world. We must ask the question, as Burge articulates, "What is the voice of God in the circumstances that surround us?" As we seek to discern God's purposes, our view of the world expands beyond our private experiences: "The study of the Scriptures opens one up to see a global mission of God inside of the world." For Burge, it is this intersection of the Word and the world that compels him into action and engagement. He says, "I am not compelled to act out of my own pathos, but because I have a deeper understanding of God's perspective of the world's circumstances." This understanding compels people to engage in complex circumstances as a way of manifesting God's heart for justice.

In the late 1980s, Gary Burge led a group of college students to Israel and Palestine. It was during the first uprising, or *intifada*.

The Palestinian community in the West Bank and Gaza mobilized mass forces of popular resistance. While many activities were characterized by nonviolence, the main force of physical resistance to Israeli occupation came in the form of throwing stones at the military forces. Through encounters with this massive protest movement, Burge tells of his own personal conversion toward justice: "I was involved in witnessing the first scenes of public brutality." Prior to that, Burge described his experience in America as "pretty sterile." During the *intifada,* he saw things he had never seen before. He experienced all kinds of emotions: disbelief, anger, sorrow and compassion. As he wrestled, at times he was overwhelmed by the intensity of his response.

Upon reflection on this experience and others, Burge has identified five stages of conversion toward a biblical understanding of justice, personal engagement with people affected by injustice and advocacy on their behalf. The proclamation of the Word of God plays a part in this process and has the power to penetrate one's heart in a second conversion experience.

The first stage is often *disbelief,* or even denial. "You can't believe what just happened." One's paradigm is challenged, so that one must rearrange one's thinking or ignore the encounter with community that has taken place.

The second stage often comes quickly: *anger.* Gary describes this part of conversion toward justice as "an intense feeling that this is *not right* and *should not happen.*" In the best of circumstances, this anger is a righteous anger directed toward injustice. Witnessing injustice, however, often triggers unhealthy psychological responses. Thus, it is important for people to be self-aware and to know how their own personal histories intersect with the encounters they have experienced. Burge states, "When you get close to a justice issue, there are certain things within us that will trigger matters of your own soul." These triggers might ignite anger, pride and other destructive patterns that can inhibit the work of God. Entering into anger in a healthy way is a spiritual discipline. Burge states, "The spiritual discipline is to energize your understanding of God's plan inside of the world." This part of the process of transformation is an activity in its own right.

The third stage is *partisan activism*, in which one aligns aggressively with one side of the problem. The fuel inside the soul sometimes can further complicate problems rather than being constructive.

The fourth stage may appear as despair but also includes feeling sorry for the loss and pain in the situation. This *compassion* appears when one "stands back and looks at the whole situation." When the anger overwhelms, it has the potential to either explode or to shift toward a compassionate response.

Finally, Burge describes the final stage of conversion as a progression toward *constructive contributions*. This final stage of transformation is a movement toward peacemaking and constructive involvement in the situation.

As Burge wrestled with the complex reality of conflict in the Middle East, he directly related to the conflict from a biblical perspective. As a professor, Burge engages in proclamation through both the written and the spoken word. His books seek to proclaim truth while addressing issues from the perspective of historical justice.

Burge offers a legitimate critique of contemporary evangelicalism: "Most evangelicals are woefully inadequate at speaking comprehensively about the circumstances within which we live." Christ-followers must be willing to listen to the world with the ears of God. In writing about the cost of proclamation, Burge says, "Many of my evangelical friends look at my writings that address social issues and don't understand why I do it. They don't understand why I take the risk."

As a New Testament scholar, his study of perspectives toward the land of Israel motivated him to write *Jesus and the Land* to respond to the questions of "What land does God love?" and "Who is a child of Abraham?" As he came to understand the teachings of the Bible in response to these questions, he began to ask how this related to his own engagement in the Holy Land. His book *Whose Land? Whose Promise?* responds to the questions Burge was asking about the people living in the land.[36] Burge declares, "Those two books represent the twin pillars of engagement in my own life."

Martin Luther King Jr.'s story exemplifies this dual encounter of the integration of God's Word with the circumstances of the surrounding community, particularly for people of color in the middle of the twentieth century. King understood the politics of the South and was able to preach a gospel of freedom to all people: those who were suffering from injustice and the whites who perpetrated the violence against them. Burge describes the process of conversion for the civil rights leader: "As King preached, there was an evolution in his proclamation." One can almost visually experience the process of transformation as King spoke the Word of God and then applied it to the circumstances of his day. "In the practice of preaching, King was being transformed," Burge says. King aligned himself with the poor and "had the courage to take a very dangerous step and to proclaim God's Word about justice and freedom to the church and beyond."

CONTEMPORARY PRAXIS

Reflecting on the influence of community for King, one might ask how to live this out in terms of practical application. With the increased individualism, reliance on social media and personal isolation of the twenty-first century, true community can be difficult to find and challenging to maintain. The American rat race of busy work schedules, children's afterschool activities and church programs leaves little discretionary time for engaging in deep relationships and God-honoring friendships.

King's image of the beloved community should serve as a model for Christian communities today. Charles Marsh writes: "While the *church* as a worshipping community exists for the specific purposes of confessing, proclaiming, and worshipping Jesus Christ as Lord, the beloved community quietly moves from its historical origins into new and unexpected shapes of communion and solidarity."[37] The church, for many believers, is the primary place where Christian community is cultivated and developed.

Richard Foster claims Christian community is one of the "major weapons" in the global battle against injustice. "When I speak of 'Christian community,' I am referring not just to the work of churches, and certainly not churches as they are often manifest today," Foster writes. "I am speaking of an alternative way of living that shows forth social life as it is meant to be lived. Communities of love and acceptance. Fellowships of freedom and liberation. Centers of hope and vision. Societies of nurture and accountability. Little pockets of life and light so stunning that a watching world will declare, 'See how they love one another!'"[38]

Christian communities diligently seeking to honor God have multiple purposes. Communities gather to worship and proclaim the truth of Christ as Lord and Savior. People come together to study the Word of God and to learn together about the teachings of Scripture. Corporate prayer is not only a means of drawing the community closer together but also of connecting the group with the heart of God. Communities of Christians also provide the opportunity for fellowship and heart-to-heart connections with other people. The purpose of Christian community does not end here, however. God requires Christian community to live out the tenets of the gospel in the world: to make disciples of all nations (Matthew 28) and to respond to the needs of the least of these (Matthew 25). Evangelism and service are two critical components of God-honoring communities.

As we consider how community manifests itself in the life of the church, we would be remiss to not include a discussion of responding to the needs of others. King had strong feelings in this regard. Jackson writes: "King believed the church had the opportunity to be an incredible beacon for peace and justice."[39] Church communities must be intentional to not become insular and singularly focused. Churches can sometimes become mini-social clubs that further perpetuate one another's false ideas, cultural stereotypes and prejudices. Thus, diversity in community has great value! Community groups must be committed to holistic mission. This includes responding to one another's needs while also being engaged in social activism on behalf of others beyond their immediate sphere of contact.

When I was serving as the executive pastor of Hillside Covenant Church, I witnessed an amazing transformation. The church is up on a hill in an affluent neighborhood and in some ways very removed from the needs of people outside of the church community. As part of a new outreach initiative, several members of the church began to host neighborhood picnics in a local park. During one of those first events, people from the neighborhood joined the church community in fellowship, eating hot dogs and hamburgers and spending time together. A few of the visitors happened to be homeless.

As relationships developed, these visitors—Larry, Jon and others—were invited to attend a church event during the Christmas season. No one was sure if they would come. Walking to the church necessitates climbing a hill that sometimes feels like a small mountain. When the evening of the event arrived, Larry and Jon came. That evening marked the beginning of a significant transformation—certainly for the men who had the courage to not only climb a hill but to enter the church, but even more so for the men and women already a part of the Hillside community.

Over the next few years, deeply meaningful relationships began to develop. Laura and Tom Roy, two of the main leaders, gave of themselves greatly. While they sacrificed financially to come alongside of the homeless community in Walnut Creek, the greatest gifts they gave were their hearts and their home. In addition to weekly lunches and picnics in the park, the church began to mobilize programs of support around issues of alcohol abuse and job training. There have been some incredible success stories of individuals now gainfully employed and no longer living on the street. The challenges and disappointments along the way have also been significant, but the beauty of these encounters lies in the way the Hillside community grew as a result of being in relationship with people outside of their social and economic realm. This messy ministry is a small glimpse of the powerful work of God in the midst of beloved community.

King's call for the church to live out beloved community is a reminder of God's desire that the world be intimately connected with him and with one another. The power of God in community breaks down walls of differences that divide, whether they are financial, social, political or otherwise. The beloved community is called to live out the love of God in the world by engaging in acts of service and social change. As a proclamation of the good news, the beloved community manifests God's love to people and draws them toward the kingdom.

◆ *Small Groups*

One of the most traditional ways of engaging in the local church community is through participating in small groups. Books upon books have been written about the best way to facilitate, host, launch and grow through these little pockets of community within the church. I have been a part of a great many groups, each with their own character, purpose and functionality. Small groups can be an excellent way for new church members to be introduced to others. They can also be helpful in creating a structure that encourages studying the Word together, praying for one another's needs and developing true community.

In light of the challenge most small groups have of reaching beyond their immediate demographic circle, consider creative ways to invite others to join your group. You may want to host a study of a book such as Curtiss Paul DeYoung's *Coming Together in the 21st Century: The Bible's Message in an Age of Diversity*, which focuses on attributes of biblical community.[40]

◆ New Monasticism and Intentional Communities

All across the United States and different parts of the world, small pockets of Christians have committed to enter into life together in intimate ways. These communities take different shapes and forms. Some have covenant agreements outlining their mutual commitment to doing life together. Some live in different houses on the same block, and others share the same house and physical space. These communities often share meals, finances, care of their children, household chores, daily fellowship and worship.

These communities are not only committed to meeting their own internal needs but to positively contributing toward community transformation around them. These groups take seriously God's call to service and justice. They esteem the faith practices of hospitality and community while also physically responding to the needs of people outside of their immediate circles. They are committed to the holistic mission of the gospel, living out the core tenets of the faith in word and deed.

The New Monastics are a loose consortium of communities that have chosen to live in this type of proximity and closeness. The Simple Way in Philadelphia started out as a small intentional community and has now grown to ten houses on the same block. To some, this type of commitment to community may seem radical, but there is much we could learn from these men, women and children who have chosen to live their lives as expressions of the beloved community.

Consider reading Shane Claiborne's *The Irresistible Revolution: Living as an Ordinary Radical* or Scott Bessenecker's *The New Friars: The Emerging Movement Serving the World's Poor* to learn more.[41]

◆ *Storytelling and Proclamation*

Let Your Life Speak by Parker Palmer is a marvelous little book about vocation; the subtitle, *Listening for the Voice of Vocation,* suggests the way our very choices proclaim a message about vocation.[42] All of us, through the pursuit of our God-given vocation, have something to proclaim. The proclamation of the life of a Christian is a witness to the ministry and person of Christ. The Christian life, in word, action and deed, is a proclamation of the truth of the gospel.

One could argue that all of us play a role in proclaiming the good news of God's kingdom. As we consider community and its transforming power, the desired outcome is to serve as a witness for God's work in the world. The power of community is not simply in the fulfillment of our desire to be connected but in the mobilizing force for change that comes when communities commit to making a difference in the world.

One of the ways proclamation takes form in the context of community is storytelling. Daniel Taylor writes in *Tell Me a Story,* "And nothing will help us act confidently and effectively in the world more than the understanding that we are characters in a story that we share with other characters."[43] As we become more comfortable in sharing the work of God in our lives, our stories serve as a proclamation of God's hand and feet in action. May we, like King, commit ourselves to being both proclaimers and doers of the Word of God in the world.

5

Fairuz

From Worship to Freedom

O pure virgin rejoice and again I say rejoice.
For your Son has risen from the tomb on the third day.

"Be Enlightened," Sung By Fairuz[1]

O NE OF THE MOST POWERFUL MOMENTS of my life occurred in 2005, when I helped to lead a Justice Journey with members from Willow Creek Community Church and Salem Baptist Church in the Chicago area on a spiritual pilgrimage through the southern United States. The journey consisted of dialogue about the history of the African American experience, the civil rights movement and race in America. Our group consisted of almost forty African Americans and Caucasians who spent the week together traveling through the Deep South visiting memorials, museums and people who had been a part of the movement.

In Alabama, our group was introduced to two amazing women who had been teenagers during the voting rights protests and non-violent resistance in Selma. On March 7, 1965, a group of more than six hundred nonviolent protestors from the Student Nonviolent Co-ordinating Committee (SNCC), the Southern Christian Leadership

Conference (SCLC) and the community attempted to cross the Edmund Pettus Bridge on a march from Selma to Montgomery. En route, the protestors found their way blocked by police forces and state troopers, who ordered them to turn around. The white police force shot tear gas into the crowd and used clubs to beat back the marchers. More than fifty people were hospitalized in what came to be known as "Bloody Sunday."[2] Troy Jackson writes in *Becoming King*: "Police officers bludgeoned marchers in Selma, Alabama, when they attempted to cross the Edmund Pettus Bridge in a march to Montgomery to lobby for voting rights."[3] The two women with whom we met had been a part of the events on Bloody Sunday. Starting at Brown Chapel, Martin Luther King Jr. and hundreds of others made a second attempt on March 9, but they were forced to turn around when they got to the Edmund Pettus Bridge. Finally, on March 21, 1965, a successful march occurred under federal protection, and protestors were able to travel from Selma to Montgomery. The Voting Rights Act of 1965 passed a few months later.

During the Justice Journey in 2005, our group prepared to once again cross the Edmund Pettus Bridge, symbolizing the beginning of the historic march. As had our predecessors half a century before, our group met for worship in Brown Chapel. At one moment during our worship service Mrs. Mays, an elderly African American woman and choir member at Salem Baptist, stood up in the choir loft and began to sing:

Oh freedom, oh freedom, oh freedom over me
And before I'd be a slave I'll be buried in a my grave
And go home to my Lord and be free.

No more mourning, no more mourning, no more mourning
over me
And before I'd be a slave I'll be buried in a my grave
And go home to my Lord and be free.

No more crying, no more crying, no more crying over me
And before I'd be a slave I'll be buried in a my grave
And go home to my Lord and be free.

Oh freedom, oh freedom, oh freedom over me
And before I'd be a slave I'll be buried in a my grave
And go home to my Lord and be free.

Tears streamed down her face as she sang. Her voice was as pure as an angel's, and it resonated throughout the historic chapel. As she sang about freedom, her worship was a declaration of God's promises to his people that one day true freedom will come.

Our group, accompanied by the two women who had been present during the traumatic events of Bloody Sunday, joined arm in arm and marched from Brown Chapel across the Edmund Pettus Bridge. It was the first time those women had crossed the bridge in forty years. We sang "Ain't gonna let nobody turn me around" and other spirituals.

Songs of worship played a significant role in the civil rights movement. Mary Elizabeth King, who worked alongside of Martin Luther King Jr. (no relation) in the SNCC, writes about how the freedom songs of the civil rights movement "raised courage, stated the goals, declared commitment, united separated communities, and sometimes took melodic aim at notorious police chiefs."[4] The content of the songs often came from spirituals, which held great meaning for generations of African Americans because of the experience of slavery. King expounds: "As a contemporary expression of spirituals, freedom songs derived from the black choral tradition that developed from the African and American experiences, matured in the fires of southern slavery."[5] Through music and the acknowledgment of dependency upon God, spirituals empowered and mobilized the African American community in their quest for freedom.

For example, when Martin Luther King Jr. entered Shiloh Church in Albany, Georgia, in 1961, "the crowd came to its feet cheering, and spontaneously launched into a joyous song of greeting, 'Free-dom, Free-dom, Free-dom,' one of the many expressions of hope and commitment that the people of Albany brought forth to sustain themselves."[6] Martin Luther King Jr. preached about the power of song as young men and women, the foot soldiers of the movement, were attacked and arrested.

And Bull Connor would tell them to send the dogs forth and they did come; but we just went before the dogs singing, "Ain't gonna let nobody turn me around" . . . And we went before the fire hoses. . . . That couldn't stop us. And we just went on before the dogs and we would look at them; and we'd go on before the water hoses and we would look at it, and we'd just go on singing "Over my head I see freedom in the air" . . . And then we would be thrown in the paddy wagons . . . and we would just go in the paddy wagon singing, "We Shall Overcome."[7]

During the movement, African Americans equated their own quest for liberation with the deliverance of the Israelites from captivity in Egypt. As Moses led the people to freedom and to the Promised Land, the spiritual music of the civil rights movement acknowledged God as the great liberator.

The civil rights movement, in large part, was launched from the pews and doorsteps of churches. Historian Henry Mitchell writes of how the lyrics of gospel songs would turn up in the most unexpected of places within the African American community. Many times, the Christian worldview is expressed "unashamedly by persons" who would not self-identify as Christians. Mitchell writes of this phenomenon: "They may not be fully believing and committed followers of Christ, but they are not very far from the Kingdom. Because the Word in Black churches is often preached and sung in familiar idiom, it is not confined within the church walls."[8] Many participants of the civil rights movement were committed followers of Christ. As they sang and marched for freedom, the words proclaimed in song were a profession of worship.

FAIRUZ

Christian worship has a long tradition of acknowledging God's attributes as Lord and Creator while also being intricately tied to people's quest for freedom and justice. This relationship is seen in the music of one of the most famous singers in the Arab world, Fairuz. Fairuz's songs have penetrated the divides of nationality and religion and become a unifying force for Maronite Christians and Arabs around the world. Maronites are an Eastern sect of the Catholic Church with ties to a fourth-century Syriac monk named Maron, who was venerated as a saint. Fairuz is a devout Maronite Christian. Two of her most famous albums, *Christmas* and *Good Friday*, are clearly expressions of her Christian devotion.

Fairuz was born as Nouhad Wadi Haddad to a Syrian Catholic father and a Maronite mother on November 21, 1935, in Lebanon. As her professional music career was launched, she took the name Fairuz, which means "turquoise" in Arabic. Over the decades of her musical career she has been called by many adoring names, such as "Neighbor to the Moon" and "Ambassador to the Stars."[9] Fairuz began her musical career as a teenager in the late 1940s, when she became a chorus girl on a Lebanese radio station.[10] Prior to that she had sung in the church choir but had not had any professional singing opportunities. Her voice and music were so powerful and distinct that she became increasingly famous and started performing all over Lebanon and the world.

Fairuz's music began to be lauded around the world and she received numerous prestigious awards for her contributions. In 1957, Lebanon's President Chamoun presented Fairuz with the Cavalier

Medal, the highest honor ever received by a Lebanese artist.[11] Similarly in 1963, King Hussein of Jordan presented her with the Medal of Honor, followed by the Gold Medal of His Majesty in 1975.[12] Today Fairuz is a cultural and political icon. She possesses a key to almost every city where she has performed. In 1968, she visited Jerusalem with her father and received one of her most prized possessions: a key to the city from the Jerusalem Cultural Committee.[13] Although Fairuz never performed in Jerusalem, many of her songs speak of the spiritual significance and the suffering of the people of the city, known in Arabic as "Al Quds."

Fairuz sings many folk songs that laud her native country of Lebanon. In 1969, however, Fairuz's songs were banned from radio stations for six months because she refused to sing at a private concert in honor of Algerian President Houari Boumedienne. The incident only served to increase her popularity throughout Lebanon. Fairuz made it clear she was always willing to sing to the public and to various countries and regions, but she would never sing to any individual. As a result of this incident, by the 1970s, Fairuz came to be known as "the Soul of Lebanon" because of her nationalistic commitments.[14]

During the Lebanese civil war (1975-1990), Fairuz refused to perform for one political party or another, believing such a performance could further incite sectarian divisions.[15] As a result, she was banned from singing publicly for a season, but her popularity throughout the Arab world only grew stronger because of her personal convictions. She also feared that the Maronite emphasis of some of the folk songs she sang was not representative of the cultural diversity of Lebanon and that the content could be particularly volatile considering the nature of the war.[16] As her fame grew, the most creative poets of the Arab world rushed to compose lyrics to be interpreted by her voice. Dozens of famous poets and artists have written lyrics for Fairuz. By the twenty-first century, she had performed or recorded more than eight hundred different songs.[17]

Fairuz's acclaim has largely been unrivaled. She performed concerts at the Royal Festival Hall in London that reached record-breaking sales at the box office—more than when Frank Sinatra had been in town. Fairuz has performed all over the world at the most prestigious venues, including the Albert Hall, Carnegie Hall, Lincoln Center and Salle Pleyel, among many others.[18]

PIETY AND FAITH

Fairuz's professional vocation is that of a singer and not a leader of worship. Nonetheless, her relationship with God has been a source of strength and centeredness for her heart for justice. Much of her music is Christ-centered. Her hymns, particularly those sung at Christmas and Easter, are beautiful expressions of the spiritual discipline of worship. She has other songs that include lyrics that clearly call for freedom and justice.

Fairuz lives a very private life. Nonetheless, those around her clearly witness expressions of her faith in her daily activities. Throughout her career, people reported that she could often be found kneeling in a posture of prayer somewhere in the vicinity of the recording studio.[19] Largely influenced by her youth in a devout Melkite household, Fairuz's personal expressions of piety were often ascetic in manner.[20] Fairuz weekly attends mass in the village church at Antilias.[21] Every year during Holy Week, she shares the gift of song and leads the congregation of devout villagers by singing well-known hymns and songs of worship. In April 2005, Fairuz performed Good Friday Mass at the Church of the Lady of Mu-haidseh in Bikfayaa, a summer resort east of Beirut.[22] It is said that her worship not only "affirmed the audience's belief in the cruci-fixion, but also in the rising of Christ."[23] One witness identified Fairuz as an "ambassador of heaven" who knelt at the altar with her head bowed in supplication as her voice filled the small church.[24]

WORSHIP

Fairuz's two most famous albums of worship are her recordings for Christmas and Good Friday. Her music has had significant influence in telling people the story of Christ. It is hard to explain the power of her music and the penetrating qualities of her voice. Her Christmas and Good Friday hymns are sung in Arabic. The language is poetic and powerful.

One of the Eastern hymns is called *"Almasiho Qam"* in Arabic, which means "Christ Has Risen."[25] The words of the song proclaim the truth of Christ's resurrection:

Christ has risen from the dead, and by His death . . . He trampled death. And those in the tombs, He granted them eternal life. This is the day which the Lord has made, let us rejoice and be glad in it.

The words of this hymn are simple in content and yet overwhelmingly powerful, particularly when set to music.[26] Another example of a song of worship is called *"Esta-niri"* in Arabic, or "Be Enlightened."[27] The words go something like this:

The angel came to the one who is full of grace. O pure virgin rejoice and again I say rejoice. For your Son has risen from the tomb on the third day. Be enlightened, O New Jerusalem. For the glory of God has shown upon you. Now rejoice and be glad O Jerusalem. And you, O pure one, O Mother of God, sing for your Son's resurrection.

Throughout Jerusalem, Bethlehem and Arab communities around the world, the songs of Fairuz can be heard during the seasons of Advent and Lent.

THE CITY OF JERUSALEM

Jerusalem holds a special place in Fairuz's heart and music. Many of her songs speak about the spiritual significance of the Holy City.

Fairuz also sings songs that cry out on behalf of the suffering of the city and the people of Jerusalem. The song "*Ya Zahrat al Madayn,*" or "Flower of the Cities," is a famous song that talks about how the Arab community of Jerusalem suffered during the 1948 war. The song addresses the significance of the city of Jerusalem to the three Abrahamic faiths: Christianity, Islam and Judaism. The words speak of the city and its people:

> It is for you O city that I pray. . . . It is for you O splendid home, O Flower of the Cities . . . O Jerusalem, O Jerusalem, O Jerusalem. Our eyes are set out to you every day. . . . They walk through the porticos of the temples, embrace of the old churches, and take the sadness away from the mosques. O night . . . O path of those who left for the sky, our eyes are set out to you every day and I pray.
>
> The child is in the cave and his mother is Miriam, two faces crying. For those who roamed, for the children without houses, for those who resisted and were martyred at the gates. And the peace was martyred in the homeland of peace. And the law tumbled at the gates of the city, when Jerusalem city fell. Love left and in the heart of the world the war was settled. The child is in the cave and his mother is Miriam, two faces crying and I pray.[28]

The song continues with prayers for peace and the liberation of Jerusalem. In the song, the city of Jerusalem is esteemed and lauded.

MUSIC AS A CRY FOR JUSTICE

Fairuz's songs of freedom take on more significant meaning in light of the 2011 Arab revolutions. Beginning with Tunisia and spreading throughout Egypt, nonviolent resistance against oppressive government regimes sprang up across the Middle East. Later popular resistance, particularly in Libya and Syria, became very violent. Many of the protestors faced severe violence and even overt military responses from their country's ruling parties. Libya's battles almost became a civil war, and hundreds were killed. Violence claimed lives from Bahrain to Yemen. The violence of the Assad regime in Syria was among the worst. In the summer of 2011, *New York Times* reporter Anthony Shadid reported that a song, "Come on Bashar, Leave," swept across Syria and boldly called for the President Bashar al-Assad to step down.[29] Reminiscent of the slave spirituals resurrected in the American civil rights movement, songs in the Arab world hold deep meaning and are often used as prophetic utterances in people's quests for freedom and independence.

Mary Elizabeth King writes about communication as a fundamental need of nonviolent mobilization and organizing. Often songs capture the "nature of the specific grievance."[30] Songs of freedom hold the truth of oppression within the collective memory of the people who have suffered. Mary King continues, "The wrong that has brought people to shed passivity and actively wage the conflict without violence must be clearly grasped, if success is to be achieved."[31]

American hip hop is another genre of music that expresses the angst of the African American community. Recently, I was introduced to the hip hop movement that has been emerging among the Palestinian population in Israel, the West Bank and Gaza. *Slingshot Hip Hop* (2008) is a documentary film about several hip hop groups that began in the 1990s. The Palestinian hip hop group DAM, from Lod, Israel, recorded a song called "Who's the Terrorist?" that has more than a million hits on YouTube. DAM represents the Arabic word for "eternity." The hip hop genre, in Israel and around the world, has attracted a younger generation of followers who desire to use music to call out injustice.

More familiar to the American Christian audience are many traditional evangelical hymns that play a similar role of identifying injustice and calling people to repentance. "Amazing Grace," one of the most well-known hymns in the world, was written by the reformed slave trader John Newton. The words of the famous hymn were motivated by Newton's deep convictions about the horror of his own role in the African slave trade: "Amazing grace, how the sweet the sound, that saved a wretch like me. I once was lost, but now am found, was blind but now I see."[32] In 1755, Newton left the slave trade and eventually became an Anglican minister. Newton's hymns contribute to the long tradition of worship as a means of calling people to repentance and speaking out against injustice.

While it is important to distinguish worship and the use of music for the proclamation of justice, these two concepts are interconnected. Isaiah 58 details what God considers "true worship." Similarly, Amos 5 speaks of God's rejection of the worship life of the Israelites: "I hate, I despise your religious festivals; your assemblies are a stench to me" (Amos 5:21). Richard Foster asks why God would reject the worship of his people and responds: "One reason, and one reason alone, accounted for God's forthright rejection of their religious devotion: all of the festivals, all of the sacrifices, all of the instruments and music of worship failed because they were not accompanied by acts of justice and righteousness."[33] The words of the prophet Amos continues with powerful imagery of God's heart in this regard: "But let justice roll on like a river, righteousness like a never-failing stream" (Amos 5:24).

The Quakers' emphasis on justice derives from their understanding of Christian worship. James White writes: "Since the Quaker movement in the seventeenth century, there has been a strong awareness among the Friends that worship must not marginalize anyone because of sex, color, or even servitude." Thus in Quaker circles during colonial American history and throughout the following centuries, white men and women worshiped and proclaimed the presence of God side by side with slaves and people of color. Limitations were not imposed on who would lead, preach, speak and proclaim the Word of God. While most of the rest of

America placed restrictions in worship on "an exclusively white male prerogative," the community of Friends modeled inclusivity in worship.[34] Today, Friends communities continue to practice an inclusive form of worship.

Worship

How do Christians define worship? Certainly the spiritual discipline of worship is more than simply singing songs about God on a Sunday morning. The corporate act of musical worship brings glory to God and, thus, is important. A deeper understanding of the meaning of Christian worship, however, is helpful. Orthodox theologian George Florovsky defines worship as "the response of men [sic] to the Divine call, to the 'mighty deeds' of God, culminating in the redemptive act of Christ."[35] Roman Catholic theology contains a simpler understanding of worship: "the glorification of God and the sanctification of man [sic]."[36] Luther, father of the Protestant Reformation, defines worship this way: "that nothing else be done in it than that our dear Lord Himself talk (*rede*) to us through His holy word and that we, in turn, talk (*reden*) to him in prayer and song of praise."[37] Luther seeks worship as a sort of communication—a call and response—between God and his people. In response to Luther, James White, in his *Introduction to Christian Worship*, concludes, "Thus worship has a duality, revelation and response—both of them empowered by the Holy Spirit."[38]

Contemporary worship takes many different forms. Beyond musical expression, other forms of worship include creative use of the arts such as painting, photography, drama, poetry and dance. These expressions are ways people ascribe to God the truth of his character and attributes of who he is and what he has done. The names of God expressed in the Holy Scripture provide fodder for worship: *Jehovah* (the I AM), *Emmanuel* (God with us), *El Shaddai* (God Almighty), *Elohim* (God the Creator), to name a few. Worth is ascribed to God because of his many attributes, including goodness, magnanimity, holiness, kindness, purity, power, generosity and love.

◆ Attributes of God

Perhaps you have seen one of the many posters that identify the names of God found in the Bible and their meanings. The names of God can be further inspiration for this activity. This exercise can be done using different mediums. Start with a blank sheet of paper and some writing utensils such as crayons, markers, oil crayons or charcoals. You might consider using paint or watercolors instead. Enter your time in prayer by invoking God's presence. Spend time creating pictures, symbols, words or whatever comes to mind as you prayerfully reflect upon the attributes of God. Ask God to reveal himself to you as you worship. When you are finished, close your time by dedicating your art to God in prayer. If you feel comfortable, share your creation with someone close to you and talk about ways you experienced God as you created the piece.

LITURGY

Liturgy, in the context of corporate church services, is an important component of worship. James White talks about two key aspects of worship: structures and services. Structures include things such as the liturgy or calendar for organizing a year's worship. Liturgy may be understood as a particular order of public service or worship sanctioned by the church. Liturgy may include some of the outward and visible forms such as instrumental music, songs of praise to God and different forms of art.[39] James White expands our understanding of communal worship: "Liturgy, then, is a work performed by the people for the benefit of others. In other words, it is the quintessence of the priesthood of believers that the whole priestly community of Christians shares."[40] In other words, liturgy is an opportunity for private worship to become a corporate encounter, in which people can use their gifts to contribute to the communal experience of worshiping God.

Worship services sometimes include practices and rituals of observation such as the Lord's Supper.[41] Rituals can be understood as
behavior that has abiding characteristics. By nature, ritual is re-
petitive and serves some communal function.[42] Liturgical scholars
tend to think of worship as "core Christian patterns" that might
include: "Sunday and the week, the service of word and table,
praise and beseeching, teaching and bath, and the year and Pascha
(Easter)."[43] Communion and baptism are important components
of communal worship experiences because of the enduring nature
of these ritualistic acts.

SACRAMENTS

Sacraments play a significant role in Christian worship. They are
an outward action or representation of worship. Sacraments are
an "outward sign of an inward grace." White reminds us of the
role the sacraments play as they call us to "'Taste and see,' to
touch, to hear, even to smell 'that the Lord is good' (Psalm
34:8)."[44] The Roman Catholic Church acknowledges seven sacraments, whereas Protestants generally only acknowledge two:
baptism and the Lord's Supper.[45]

In the eighteenth century, the Christian community began to transition in their understanding of sacraments. Sacraments came to
mean less about God's mysterious intervention and presence in sacra-
mental acts and more about humanity's response. Sacraments came
to be understood as an encouragement to lead a better life: "The sacraments were occasions for humans to remember what God had done
in times past. They were credited with immense practical value in
stirring up humans to greater moral endeavor," writes White.[46]

Christian traditions have different understandings of worship in
light of liturgy and sacraments. Some denominations are considered
"high church" and use a more structured liturgy in their worship.

Other denominations do not approach worship from a structural perspective. Christian tradition, from Orthodoxy to Catholicism to Protestantism, expresses worship in profoundly different ways.

The sacrament of Communion is particularly relevant for laborers of justice because of its symbolic significance as an act of reconciliation. Through receipt of the Eucharist, we acknowledge, individually and corporately, sin and brokenness in the world. By accepting the sacrament, a person confesses the role of Christ's death on the cross for individual and corporate atonement. This symbolic action marks the reconciliation of Christ-followers to God and humankind. In its purest form, the Eucharist is an act of humble worship that reconciles people to God and community.

WENCHE MIRIAM: MINISTRY AND WORSHIP

Wenche Miriam came to the United States in 1989 from Norway expecting to only stay a year. More than twenty years later, she looks back and is reminded that God had a plan for her that was different from her own. From the time she was five years old, singing had been a big part of her life. Miriam describes her childhood: "When given the opportunity, I would jump up being the microphone and sing my heart out."[47] Throughout her youth, Wenche sang in choirs and youth groups. After coming to the U.S., she began to sing in churches in the Bay Area and in Seattle. Today she works full-time as the financial comptroller for a private Christian foundation. She is also the executive director of a nonprofit organization called Ministry & Worship, Inc., which she founded in 2010.

Wenche Miriam describes her ministry of worship as "singing and learning to completely surrender to the experience of letting God lead." For Wenche, worship with music has been her personal way of connecting with God. She believes that "entering into a place of worship can be done any time of day or night" and should be a part of our daily worship and spiritual discipline. She has often been called to step outside of her comfort zone, which demands that she trust in God as she seeks to honor him in her ministry. In this spirit, Miriam decided to go to a prison ministry orientation program at the church she was attending. She describes the experience, "Listening to what was said . . . it blew me away!" She was deeply moved by the stories of and interviews with incarcerated men and women about how they had ended up behind bars. Miriam realized that she was "no different than many of them." She felt deep pain and sorrow to see that many incarcerated men and women had been abandoned by their families. With all of this in mind, Miriam signed up for her first prison visit as a part of the church's worship team. She knew she had music to share and that leading worship was something she could do to offer encouragement and care.

Miriam describes the feelings she had when she first began ministry in the prisons and jails: "The thought of me walking into the prison and speaking to women and men behind bars was terrifying at first. . . . What could I possibly say or do that would make any difference?" Miriam describes submitting her insecurities to God and making the choice to "get out of the boat" as Peter did on the Sea of Galilee. After spending time in relationship with some of the men and women in prison, Miriam realized they were lonely and hurting. She heard the stories of men and women who had grown up in poverty, suffered mistreatment from their parents, been beaten and sexually molested, abused drugs and alcohol: the list goes on and on. She experienced deep compassion for these men and women and committed to walking with them.

Miriam pursued ministry within the prison system because she understood that incarcerated men and women needed the grace of God. She says, "After my first few visits into the prisons, I had the courage to be more involved. I learned the true meaning of leading worship." The more she spent time with the incarcerated, the more she realized how the love of God can be both expressed and experienced when people worship him. As inmates expressed the desire and hunger to be closer to God, Wenche grew in her ability to lead them in worship. As she continued to lead worship within the prison system, she realized that part of her calling was to walk with incarcerated men and women on their journey.

In 2009, Miriam participated in a ministry trip to Louisiana State Penitentiary at Angola and Louisiana Correctional Institute for Women to learn about the reform that can take place behind the walls of prison. She tells of the experience, "I received so much more than I could possibly have understood at the time. It changed my life in ways I never dreamed of." After hearing her sing, one of the inmates encouraged her to pray about starting a ministry of music. This was the beginning of Ministry & Worship, Inc. The purpose of the ministry is to "be a tool to bring the love of Christ to people behind bars and their families through fellowship, music and community awareness."

Today, Wenche Miriam continues to be a lover of Christ and a leader of worship. She describes her own journey of faith: "My faith can be summarized in one word. His name is Jesus. . . . I was once a prisoner. No, I did not live behind steel bars . . . but I lived in a cell of my own making. I was incarcerated by feelings of failure, loneliness and the sense that I could never measure up. When I could not get myself out, God came in."

Wenche is deeply committed to her family. In addition to her work and taking care of her husband and son, she continues to worship. Through her experiences in the prisons she has learned: "Worship leading is music, dance, smiles, joy, tears, truth, cries for help and words . . . words of compassion, words of love and words of justice!"

CONTEMPORARY PRAXIS

"I am the vine; you are the branches. If you remain in me and I in you, you will bear much fruit; apart from me you can do nothing" (Jn 15:5). In worship, Christians have the opportunity to remain in Christ as represented by John 15. In the Gospel of John, the Greek word for "remaining" is μένω (*menō*). Worship is an expression of the intimacy we experience with God when we remain (μένω) in him. Rory Noland, worship leader and mentor to artists, writes: "Abiding in Christ means that we are in right relationship with Him, that we're growing in Him, that our lives reflect His love, and that our hearts are full of His Word."[48] We respond by lauding God through our worship and response.

All people, regardless of their level of artistic talent, can be worshipers of God. Some people, however, are more gifted than others! Creative forms of worship can include various artistic expressions such as the visual arts, worship, drama, poetry or dance. Rory Noland reminds us that art can make a powerful impact if it is "produced with the anointing power of the Holy Spirit."[49] A leader of worship helps to create an environment in which people are reminded of the nature of God and are free to respond with praise and adoration.

In *The Heart of the Artist: A Character-Building Guide for You and Your Ministry Team*, Noland reminds us that artists have a unique understanding of discipline and the faith practice of worship. Disciplines do not have to be torturous or painful in order to be productive. Just as a classically trained pianist works for hours to master a new piece, we can also benefit from hard work. Nonetheless, artists can often uniquely appreciate the beauty of a transformative process that discipline helps to facilitate.

We have a lot to learn from artists. Noland reminds us that artists often have a keen sensitivity to God and to the suffering of humankind: "For this reason artists very often speak out against injustice, inequality, and hypocrisy. They take up the cause of those who are suffering. They make us sensitive to the lost and lonely and to the plight of the downtrodden."[50] Because of their sensitivity to people who are suffering, artists can help us to better understand how to faithfully respond to God in righteous worship. This is beneficial to understand as we reflect on what the Bible teaches about the integration of worship and justice, present in passages such as Isaiah 58.

Many Christians use their art as a means of worship and a way to boldly speak out against injustice. Consider Tim Hughes's worship song "God of Justice," which acknowledges Jesus as the rescuer of the weak and the poor and also calls the church to action: "We must go . . . live to feed the hungry . . . stand beside the broken . . . We must go."[51] Bono, one of the most famous musician-activists and lead singer of U2, often uses his platform to talk about God's heart for the poor and to speak out against global injustices. As one of the keynote speakers at the National Prayer Breakfast in 2006, Bono spoke out boldly on international issues such as poverty and AIDS. He affirmed the church and Christian community for the work they had done in mobilizing people to respond to global needs: "When churches . . . started organizing, petitioning, and even the most unholy of acts . . . lobbying on AIDS and global health, governments listened and acted. . . .You changed minds; you changed policy; and you changed the world."[52] In addition to music, film often links worship and the arts to mobilize action toward societal change. EthnoGraphic Media and its president, Bill Oechsler, have created numerous Christian films highlighting issues of injustice, including *Beyond the Gates of Splendor* (2002); *End of the Spear* (2006); *Miss HIV* (2007); and *Little Town of Bethlehem* (2010).[53] These are just a few small examples of Christians using art to both bring adoration to God through worship and to call awareness to injustice and needs in the world. As the stories of Lebanese singer Fairuz and worship leader Wenche Miriam exemplify, worship in the form of music can be a powerful tool of sharing the gospel message while also uttering cries against injustice. Music is not the only medium through which creative artists express glory to God and prophetically share messages about the condition of the world. All people, regardless of creative aptitude, can enter into these individual and corporate worship experiences through participation and witness. The goal of prophetic Christian worship is for God to be glorified and truth professed.

◆ Worship Nights

"Sing and make music from your heart to the Lord" (Eph 5:19). Throughout the Scriptures and in churches around the world and across the millennia, Christians have used song as a way of worshiping the Lord. Musical worship is a corporate expression of adoration and exultation. Dietrich Bonhoeffer reminded us: "The new song is sung first in the heart. Otherwise it cannot be sung at all. The heart sings because it is overflowing with Christ. That is why all singing in the church is a spiritual performance. Surrender to the Word, incorporation in the community, great humility, and much discipline—these are the prerequisites of singing together."[54]

Consider organizing a night at your church or in your home focused on communal worship, particularly as a means of connecting with God and propelling the community toward action and service. Invite artists to come and share their talents—poetry, film, painting, music—as a means of spending time together. The artists might have the opportunity to share about passions God has put on their hearts in terms of caring for the sick, elderly, poor or hurting in the community. Your time can be extemporaneous or planned. In addition to discerning the presence of God through the arts, also include elements of prayer and readings from Scripture. Consider using a resource such as Nancy Beach's *An Hour on Sunday: Creating Moments of Transformation and Wonder.*[55]

◆ Spiritual Art Journaling

I am not the most creative person. When I attempt to draw a picture of an animal, it looks more like an amoeba. Nonetheless, I have found art journaling to be a helpful faith practice. Instead of having a journal in which you write down thoughts and ideas, start a notebook (or use loose sheets of paper) where you can creatively express yourself through art about God. This is a form of worship. One possibility is to use Psalms as your guide. I have an art notebook that was once full of blank pages. I dedicated a single page to each of the psalms in the Scriptures. Periodically, I enter into worship by drawing pictures, designs and creative doodles that come to mind as I pray through the specific psalm for that day. Other possibilities for scriptural reflection include Leviticus 25 (drawing pictures of what the year of Jubilee or biblical *shalom* ["peace"] might look like), and Revelation 7 (in which John tells his readers about what the throne of heaven will be like when there is no injustice or brokenness in the world).

◆ Spiritually Guided Tours

God reveals himself in many ways throughout his creation. Nature is one of the most obvious ways we can see the hand of God in the world. Spiritually guided tours through nature parks, botanic gardens or art museums are wonderful ways to experience God. Just as God reveals himself through nature and creation, attributes of his disposition are also revealed through the creative expression of humans. Art museums or photo galleries are great places to better understand and experience God.

Consider hosting or inviting a spiritual director to lead a nature tour as a prayerful worship experience. Gather your small group or a few friends to enter into the experience together. Begin your time by invoking God's presence and ask that God would reveal himself to you on your walk. Read passages of Scripture that talk about God's presence in creation before you begin. As you travel, point out things to one another that call your attention to God and his character. At the close of your time, debrief about the things you have seen and experienced.

6

Desmond Tutu

FROM SABBATH TO RECONCILIATION

*All over this magnificent world God calls us to extend His kingdom of
shalom—peace and wholeness—of justice, of goodness, of compassion, of caring, of sharing, of laughter, of joy, and of reconciliation.
God is transfiguring the world right this very moment through us
because God believes in us and because God loves us.*

DESMOND TUTU[1]

As I REFLECT ON THE NECESSITY OF REST, I am aware of
the irony that I have just completed three days of intensive meetings
at work. My days started before 6:00 a.m., and I got home (on av-
erage) around 8:30 p.m. While I spent a few moments here and
there with family, I had to do work in the evenings, which kept me
up past 1:00 a.m. almost every night. This week was unique. Or at
least that's what I tell myself. We, as advocates of justice, are doing
important work—striving together, under the direction of our
godly convictions, to try to make a difference in the world. What
time is there to rest?

Looking at the creation story in Genesis, I don't think God rested on the seventh day because he was tired. We are told: "God had finished the work he had been doing; so on the seventh day he rested from all his work" (Gen 2:2). Why did he rest? What is the significance of sabbath in our work, ministry and daily lives? Scripture says God blessed the seventh day and made it holy (Gen 2:3). What is the relationship between sabbath and shalom? Is the sabbath simply about worship? Or is rest important, too? As we live out our Christian faith in the world, how important is observation of the sabbath and regular rhythms of rest and retreat? These are important questions.

Followers of different Abrahamic traditions observe sabbath as a time of worship and rest. The word sabbath comes from the Hebrew word *Shabbat* and refers to a weekly day of rest and spiritual observation. Many followers of the Jewish faith observe the sabbath regularly. In Jerusalem and other cities throughout modern-day Israel, most of the local businesses are closed from sundown on Friday until Saturday evening. One aspect of the tradition sometimes includes strict observance of God's commandment to not work during the sabbath. For example, elevators in many Jewish hotels will stop on every floor in the hotel so that patrons do not have to push a button to determine their floor of departure. I have heard stories about how, in the Old City of Jerusalem during the early twentieth century, Muslim and Christian residents would often visit their Jewish neighbors to light candles for them during Shabbat evenings. The Jewish tradition takes seriously God's commandment to rest during the sabbath. A small segment of the Christian population around the world also practices strict observation of the sabbath.

Old Testament scholar John Walton from Wheaton College takes the Genesis creation narrative beyond the initial reading of sabbath and defines it as setting the stage for cosmic worship.

Walton expounds on twenty different theological propositions of Genesis 1 in his book *The Lost World of Genesis One: Ancient Cosmology and the Origins Debate.* The cosmos functions by paralleling aspects of the temple or tabernacle, in which God is at the center, with the throne of creation where God is worshiped.[2] The Genesis account provides a glimpse of God's view of biblical shalom, in which the world will be made right as God intended it to be. Observation of the sabbath is one of the mechanisms God uses as a part of the process of restoring shalom.

DESMOND TUTU

Desmond Mpilo Tutu's life and ministry have focused on the restoration of shalom to South Africa and the world. From 1986 to 1996, Tutu served as the Anglican archbishop of Cape Town, South Africa. Tutu received global acclaim because of his efforts to end apartheid in South Africa. He has committed his life to advocating for human rights around the world and working to end the suffering of oppressed people. He has committed his life to restoring shalom: the way God intended for the world to be. His work and ministry remind us of God's radical love and call to forgiveness as a means of reconciliation. Desmond Tutu's ministry and writing emphasizes the importance of spending time with God, observing the sabbath and restoring shalom as ways to both receive and incarnate the love of Christ.

For nearly half a century, from 1948 to 1994, apartheid existed in South Africa as a government-enforced system of racial segregation. In 1948, the established apartheid system distinguished four racial groups in South Africa: coloured (blacks), natives, Asians and whites.[3] Afrikaners, a primarily Dutch minority in South Africa, enforced a system of white supremacy that caused great suffering to other racial groups, primarily blacks. Thousands of South African blacks suffered from forced removal out of city centers into urban ghettos. South African blacks, considered inferior by white South Africans, were forced to work as cheap labor and were segregated from whites. Apartheid was a systematic regime that perpetuated violence and gross injustices toward people who were not white. Desmond Tutu was born into a poor family under this system. He grew up in an apartheid ghetto under tight governmental restrictions and injustice.[4]

DISMANTLING APARTHEID

Along with many other South African leaders, including Nelson Mandela, Desmond Tutu played a significant role in dismantling apartheid. The regime was acknowledged as a "crime against humanity" as far back as 1973, but it took another twenty years before it would be dismantled.[5] Along the way, through the support of sanctions and other tactics, Tutu was a voice speaking boldly about God's love and justice. He reminded the world that God cares deeply for people who are suffering oppression. In 1984, Tutu was awarded the Nobel Peace Prize in recognition of his involvement in the nonviolent campaign for the rights of black people.[6]

Tutu described the success of Nelson Mandela in the 1994 South African presidential elections as nothing short of miraculous. People stood in long lines, whites and blacks side by side. It is difficult to grasp the significance of blacks, whites, colored, Indians, farmers, laborers, educated and unschooled standing shoulder to shoulder to vote in national elections after the fall of apartheid. Tutu described the scene as an "earth-shattering discovery" in which South Africans realized that they had more in common than differences and that "skin color and race were indeed thoroughly irrelevant."[7]

According to Tutu, people entered the voting booth "one person and emerged on the other side a totally different person."[8] This process of liberation was true for both blacks and whites. For blacks, the opportunity to vote served as a means of restoring dignity. Whites felt a relief from guilt they experienced. Tutu describes the process of a black woman emerging from the voting booth: She said, "Hey, I'm free—my dignity has been restored, my humanity has been acknowledged. I'm free!"[9]

The overturning of systemic apartheid was a liberating experience for all South Africans regardless of color, position or privilege. Whites were liberated from the role of abusing power and privilege; blacks were given physical and social freedom. The 1994 elections did not instantaneously make right the decades of racial disparity, hatred and suffering. The elections were, however, a significant turning point that launched the process of deep healing and reconciliation, which extended to greater depths that would have ever been thought possible. The end of apartheid was a critical point in restoring shalom to the people of South Africa.

Truth and Reconciliation Commission

After the end of the apartheid system, Desmond Tutu played an important role through his work as the chair of the Truth and Reconciliation Commission. One of Tutu's greatest contributions was his understanding that peace with the past could be made through confession and forgiveness of wrongs. Tutu believed: "True reconciliation is never cheap, because it is based on forgiveness, which is costly."[10] It was important to acknowledge and confess the harsh realities of the past so that forgiveness could occur and reconciliation could be pursued.

The Truth and Reconciliation Commission was a critical component of South Africa's healing from the harsh devastation of apartheid. The purpose of the commission was "to move beyond the cycles of retribution and violence that had plagued so many other countries during their transitions from oppression to democracy."[11] The commission provided the opportunity for perpetrators of political crimes to acknowledge their actions, ask for forgiveness and appeal for amnesty. Some took advantage of this opportunity, and others did not. This process offered a chance for forgiveness and healing for those who perpetrated the apartheid system while allowing those who suffered pain under the regime the chance to unburden themselves by sharing about their experiences.[12] The commission, under Tutu's leadership, helped South Africans enter into this important process of reconciliation.

Tutu believed reconciliation couldn't occur without confession and forgiveness: "True reconciliation is based on forgiveness, and forgiveness is based on true confession, and confession is based on penitence, on contrition, on sorrow for what you have done."[13] Without this process, the healing and reconciliation needed as a result of decades of oppression could not occur.

Bishop Tutu believes forgiveness is necessary because, in his words, it "gives us the capacity to make a new start."[14] The confession of wrongdoing provides an acknowledgment that someone has fallen or failed. When someone says, "Please forgive me," she or he is admitting a shortcoming and committing to not remain in that place. Forgiveness is necessary for both the perpetrator and the victim. It is a door to healing that allows the rest of the process of reconciliation to continue.

Bishop Tutu reminds his readers that confession is not the end of the process. He says, "Most frequently, the wrong has affected the victim in tangible, material ways."[15] For example, under apartheid, whites had enormous financial and material privileges. Victims were deprived financially, materially and socially as a part of their ongoing exploitation. Tutu continues: "If someone steals my pen and then asks me to forgive him, unless he returns my pen the sincerity of his contrition will be considered nil."[16] The process of reparations is an important one that helps give credence to the authenticity of confession. Tutu says, "Confession, forgiveness, and reparation, wherever feasible, form part of a continuum."[17]

The continuum is not a perfect progression, but does provide a mechanism of understanding the process of reconciliation. God's sabbath and Jubilee laws also demand reconciliation for the gross economic differentials caused by earthly injustice. Bishop Tutu's ministry is a reminder that true reconciliation cannot happen apart from God. God, the Creator of the universe, is the source of reconciliation and shalom, first and foremost to himself through Jesus: "For if, while we were God's enemies, we were reconciled to him through the death of his Son, how much more, having been reconciled, shall we be saved through his life!" (Rom 5:10). Christians believe that Christ's death on the cross was the ultimate act of reconciliation and restoration of shalom. The debt of the sins of humankind was paid through Christ's blood shed on the cross.

God's Love

Bishop Tutu's unique contributions to South Africa and the movement to end apartheid were inspired by his spiritual convictions and faith in God. Tutu believed wholeheartedly in God as Emmanuel, "God with us." He described his Creator as: "The God who is there with us in the muck. God does not take our suffering away, but He bears it with us and strengthens us to bear it."[18] This incarnational God, through the person of Jesus, offers hope in the midst of the worst suffering. God's love allows us to maintain hope that we, and the world, can be transformed.

God's love is the beginning and the end of our human experience. Observation of the sabbath, through stewardship of our time and resources, is one of the main faith practices that connect us to the love of God and his relationship with creation. While we might feel vulnerable and helpless, God's love sustains us in the midst of it. Tutu acknowledges the truth of human vulnerability and frailty because "vulnerability is the essence of creaturehood."[19]

As creatures, however, we are never helpless. We are never without God's love. And because of God's love, we are invincible. Tutu reminds us, "Our God does not forget those who are suffering and oppressed."[20] God loves us. God is with us. God sustains us.

For Tutu, not only is God with us here on earth, but Christians also have the support of one another. This "oneness" of humanity is understood in South African culture as *ubuntu*, or the community of creation. *Ubuntu* in Nguni languages, or *botho* in Sotho, is difficult to translate but refers generally to the African recognition of human interdependence with one another. Tutu writes about how *ubuntu* provides "self-assurance that comes from knowing that one belongs in a greater whole."[21]

This concept sounds markedly similar to 1 Corinthians 12, which speaks of the body having many parts. When one part of the body suffers, the whole body is diminished. Similarly, the idea of *ubuntu* reminds people that they are a part of something bigger than themselves. It provides resilience and enables people to "survive and emerge still human despite all efforts to dehumanize them."[22] One of the greatest pains of apartheid was its dehumanizing effects upon the majority population of blacks and other nonwhites in South Africa. Women and children were among those who suffered the most.

One of Tutu's greatest legacies is his advocacy of women. He speaks passionately to this issue: "Ending sexism and including women fully in every aspect of society not only ends its own great evil—the oppression of women—but also is part of the solution to the rest of the world's problems."[23] Tutu has identified gender inequality not only as a part of the South African apartheid regime but also as one of the world's greatest problems. "Until women are deeply involved in opposing the violence in the world, we are not going to bring it to an end," he asserts. "All women must be equally at the forefront of the movements for social justice."[24]

SABBATH AND SHALOM

In reflecting on reconciliation of humanity in the aftermath of apartheid, we would do well to consider a biblical understanding of God's purposes for sabbath rest and shalom. The Hebrew word *shalom* not only means "peace" but refers to a complete reconciliation of all things to God. The concept of shalom is much more than peace; it means "wholeness, completeness, harmony—the total sense of well-being, what God initially intended before the Fall—for both individuals and community."[25] Shalom is expressed in every aspect of life including the spiritual, social, economic and physical realms. Oppression is in direct opposition to shalom.

Sabbath applies to *ubuntu*, this common aspect of humanity and creation. Not only does the individual need rest and restoration; all creation requires similar sustenance that comes from God and observation of his laws. The Levitical sabbath laws commanded that the land be given rest at seven-year intervals, with no planting or harvesting or any attempt to kill insects. This would maximize productivity during other years. Just as with humans, the sabbath provided restoration and revitalization for the land.

SABBATH AND THE YEAR OF JUBILEE

Observation of the sabbath is one of the Ten Commandments given to the Israelites in the Old Testament.[26] "Observe the Sabbath day by keeping it holy, as the Lord your God has commanded you" (Deut 5:12). The idea of sabbath is relatively familiar: the people of God were to have a day of rest, dedicated to God, once a week. God established three different types of sabbaths for the people of Israel in order to teach them how to relate to one another. These sabbaths are important to the study of biblical justice, because they were the foundational laws that affected the poor.

The weekly sabbath was to be observed on the last day of the week as a day without work. This was to remind people of God's creation, when he rested on the seventh day. At the time these laws were given, Israel was an agricultural society. Taking a day off from farming the land could have significant consequences if the people did not believe that God would provide for them.

The sabbath year was to be observed after the people had worked for six years. They were to rest for the entire seventh year. This sabbath is described in Leviticus: "When you enter the land I am going to give you, the land itself must observe a Sabbath to the Lord. For six years sow your fields, and for six years prune your vineyards and gather their crops. But in the seventh year the land is to have a year of Sabbath rest, a Sabbath to the Lord" (Lev 25:2-4). Several aspects of observance characterized the sabbath year: (1) there was no work for the entire year, and the people were to live off the produce of the land; (2) all debts were forgiven; (3) those who were in slavery were set free; and (4) the law of the Lord was read to the people of Israel so they would be reminded that God was their provider and the land belonged to him. Again, the only way the people of Israel could obey the sabbath law was if they trusted God to provide for their needs.

The year of Jubilee was consecrated as a year of freedom and the year of the Lord's favor. Jubilee was the year following seven sabbath years. It was the year that proclaimed freedom for the captives, the restoration of land to its original owners and the forgiveness of debt. The Jubilee year was holy, set aside to honor God. The year of Jubilee celebrated holistic renewal for the entire community. It provided a picture of God's kingdom of justice and peace, where all things would be made right and restored to a place of shalom.

In this context, what would the people of Israel have thought when Jesus began his ministry, centuries later, with the proclamation of Isaiah declaring the year of the Lord's favor? "The Spirit of the Lord is on me, because he has anointed me to proclaim good news to the poor. He has sent me to proclaim freedom for the prisoners and recovery of sight for the blind, to set the oppressed free, to proclaim the year of the Lord's favor" (Lk 4:18-19). Jesus was declaring that his presence was the ultimate culmination of the year of Jubilee: he came to earth to bring shalom, to preach good news to the poor and to set the captives free.

SABBATH AS AN EXPRESSION OF GOD'S LOVE

Bishop Tutu's life and ministry reflect the direct link between observation of the sabbath and God's desire for justice through the end of oppression. Observation of the sabbath not only creates space for the recognition of the glory of God and the acknowledgment of his holiness, but it also highlights God's heart for justice.

Meeting with God through the practice of sabbath rest connects us to the power of God in a unique way. We must tap into the love of God in order to not hate. Sabbath reminds us both of God's holiness and of God's loving nature. Tutu manifested this powerful love of God during apartheid. After security forces carried out a massacre in Johannesburg, Archbishop Tutu "stood alone in the streets, ruined buildings all around him, and encouraged people with the words: 'Do not hate; let us choose the peaceful path to freedom.'"[27] The path to freedom cannot be pursued by hate. It must be pursued by love.

Tutu's ministry is empowered because of his deep connection with the love of God. In *Made for Goodness*, which he wrote with his daughter, Mpho, Desmond Tutu says, "Living our goodness is our way of testifying that we know ourselves to be perfectly loved by God."[28] As Christians experience the love of God, we are better able to extend that love with others. The love of God is what allows us to not see each other as enemies. Tutu warns: "When we see others as the enemy, we risk becoming what we hate. When we oppress others, we end up oppressing ourselves."[29] God's love delivers us from the need to hate and the need to objectify the other as bad or evil: as the enemy. Instead, God's love allows us to radically extend an arm of reconciliation that invites others into confession and forgiveness. The power of this type of love is beyond that which we could imagine.

The presence of shalom is not only needed within the recesses of our own hearts and minds; such restorative justice is needed throughout the world. Tutu describes the shalom of God's kingdom as one of "peace and wholeness—of justice, of goodness, of compassion, of caring, of laughter, of joy, and of reconciliation."[30] God's transformation of the world is motivated by his love for his people and his creation. The powerful and restorative love of God manifests itself in the world through Jesus and his followers. Tutu responds to the question, "What can separate us from the love of God?" He responds: "Nothing. Absolutely nothing. And as we share God's love with our brothers and sisters, God's other children, there is no tyrant who can resist us, no oppression that cannot be ended, no hunger that cannot be fed, no wound that cannot be healed, no hatred that cannot be turned to love, no dream that cannot be fulfilled."[31]

DANIEL HILL: A LIGHT IN HUMBOLDT PARK

Daniel Hill was born and raised in Chicago and now serves as the lead pastor of River City Community Church in the diverse city neighborhood of Humboldt Park. I first met Daniel when he was on staff at Willow Creek Community Church, where he served for several years under the leadership of Bill Hybels and Nancy Ortberg. Daniel was the first person who called out my gifts of leadership and gave me the opportunity to use them in the course of ministry. Daniel has an incredible ability to identify people's strengths and spiritual gifts and to utilize them for the growth and betterment of the church and community. For most of Daniel's life, he has had an understanding of God's heart for lost people: people who are apart from God and not living into the purpose of God for their lives. Midway through his ministry life, however, Daniel realized something significant was missing from his understanding of God's heart. Certainly God cares for the lost and the hurting, but God also cares deeply about the systemic issues and injustices that perpetuate oppression and brokenness. Daniel increasingly came to understand God's heart for the lost and God's heart for justice. He says, "As my theological conviction grew, I wanted to get more and more involved on the front line."[32] He became very connected to God's heart for justice through race-based issues and reconciliation.

Two primary mentors on his journey toward justice included John Perkins, founder and president emeritus of the Christian Community Development Association (CCDA), and Marian Wright Edelman, founder of the Children's Defense Fund (CDF) in Washington, D.C. Daniel became increasingly concerned and involved in justice issues around economics and education, with a significant emphasis on the effects of injustices on children. In describing this growing conviction, Daniel remembers one of Dr. Edelman's most impactful statements: "The most vulnerable group in any population is children . . . and in the U.S. the most dangerous place for a child to live is at the intersection of race and poverty." For Daniel, this quotation sums it up. The United States is the wealthiest nation in the world, and yet one out of every five children lives in poverty. This reality has severe ramifications. Daniel, through his leadership and care for the River City community, mobilizes his church to make a difference regarding poverty and education.

Daniel Hill's pastoral ministry has rested heavily on the coaching and mentorship of John Perkins of CCDA. It was a brave decision for Daniel to leave Willow Creek as a young white man and to intentionally plant a church community focused on diversity and reconciliation. Perkins told Daniel: "Don't seek to be a national leader; seek to be a light in your own community. If people outside of your community seek you out as a light, then be open to it." Thus, Daniel's ministry focuses most directly on responding to the needs of children within the community in Humboldt Park. For a child, economic stability and education are two things that allow them to flourish. Daniel says, "These two injustices [poverty and lack of access to education] stand in between a child's potential and who God created them to be. This is a horrible injustice." Education creates the opportunity for children to develop physically, emotionally and psychologically. Daniel practices a church-based justice-oriented approach. He mobilizes his church members to be advocates of justice on behalf of children at this intersection of economics and education.

Daniel knew there would be significant challenges as a white person seeking to lead a diverse community. While his faith deeply informs his understanding of justice, living out his ideals in the urban center of Chicago is another story. Often he reminds himself of the words of Hebrews 12:1-2: to "run with perseverance" and to fix one's eyes on Jesus the "pioneer and perfecter of our faith." At times he has found the myopic focus of the conservative evangelical church frustrating. Over the years, he has not lost his evangelistic zeal and desire for the gospel to reach people who are far away from God. His outreach no longer focuses merely on saving souls and drawing individuals to Jesus. Rather, an outreach-oriented evangelical emphasis must be pursued in conjunction with an understanding of God's heart for justice.

Daniel struggles with holding his understanding of "faith as an internal reality" while also focusing attention on the biblical components of righteousness and justice. He truly believes "something terrible is missing on both sides" if one focuses *only* on personal piety and righteousness or *only* on issues of justice. Thus, he has committed his pastoral ministry at River City to responding to the needs of the spiritually broken while also directly addressing injustice within the community.

River City may look like a traditional church in many regards. The congregation worships in rented space, hosts weekly Sunday worship services, and often has weekday fellowship meetings or Bible studies. However, the mission of the church extends far beyond the traditional elements of a worshiping community. River City gathers around the core values of worship, reconciliation and community development. The church, under Daniel's leadership, is committed to "see increased social and economic justice in the Humboldt Park neighborhood as well as the entire city, demonstrating compassion and alleviating poverty as tangible expressions of the Kingdom of God."[33] The congregation pays close attention to the needs of their urban community: materialism, poverty, inadequate public schools, racial disparity and economic injustice. When asked what inspired the community to engage so intentionally with their community, Daniel responds: "If we are doing justice and compassion but it is not flowing from belief in Jesus, then it is dormant, limited and finite . . . and our actions lack faith."

For Daniel, spiritual practices are critical opportunities to develop faith and encounter God. Disciplines "make us aware of frailty and sin" while providing the opportunity to "experience grace in God." As a pastor, Daniel has a special appreciation for the importance of faith and its practices. He exhorts that spiritual practices are valuable because they provide the occasion for daily mindfulness, through which we can keep our close connection to God. Spiritual practices renew our sense of forgiveness and remind us that we are sons and daughters of God. Through these disciplines, Daniel says, "we are aware of the grace of God as we are in touch with God's presence." Looking at the example of Jesus, we are reminded that he connected with God each and every morning. The

Father is at work and the Son cannot do anything without God having done it first. Justice advocates are in danger if we are not, in Daniel's words, "already participating in the work that God is doing." It is important that connection with God is the driving force for our justice-oriented action. Daniel says, "When we are renewed and refreshed in our relationship with God, it keeps our radar in order." Spiritual connection is important in order for justice activists to remain connected with the work that God is already doing.

As the lead pastor of his community, a husband and a father, Daniel Hill has many demands on his time. The observance of sabbath rest has taken on particular importance in his life and ministry. Sometimes Christians forget that observation of the sabbath is one of the Ten Commandments. Daniel often preaches on rhythms of work and the need for sabbath. In one of those sermons, Daniel said, "God knows us. He knows how we are made and knows what our weaknesses will be. And one of the great weaknesses of humanity is that we don't know how to experience rest. Despite the fact that we all long for rest—deep rest, not just a short break—few of us know how to truly experience it."[34]

Daniel's sermon included a description of two kinds of rest: (1) physical rest, and (2) soul rest. Physical rest refers to sleep and the nourishment our bodies receive when we take a break from work. The second type of rest, the rest of the soul, is a deeper necessity for the nourishment of our spirits.

Sabbath is more than simply taking a rest once out of every seven days. There is also benefit from taking rest from, as Daniel put it in his sermon, the "work of justice, the work of the church, and the work that we do for a living."[35] Every Monday, Daniel takes the day off and observes the sabbath. He spends time with his children and does things that replenish him emotionally. His rhythm also includes spending time focused on personal devel-

opment through Christian counseling. Every other week he sees a
counselor in order to analyze the health of his emotional world. He
asks the question of where he is having fear, anger and restlessness.
For Daniel, intentional focus and rest are vital components of
caring for his soul. These practices are necessary for Daniel to stay
connected to God in a durable way over time. Physical rest and
care for the soul are necessary for long-term sustainability.

Observing sabbath rest reminds Christians that we do not need
to achieve things in order to have meaningful lives. We do not have
to perform in order for God to accept us. Indeed, God's love is not
conditional upon our accomplishments or achievements. God will
keep the world running when we are willing to let it go. In other
words, observation of the sabbath is a means by which we may
"enter into the grace of God," Daniel says. We receive God's grace
and let it enter into the center of our beings. Daniel encourages
members of his congregation to practice sabbath rest as means of
taking a break from the primary type of work they do during the
week: making a living, parenting, studying or whatever the activity
might be. He encourages a mother with three kids to intentionally
take time once a week, even if it is not on a Sunday and is not for
twenty-four hours, to enter into the practice of sabbath: rest from
work and rest for the soul. This is a way that people can be reminded that God is in control. Sabbath is also a means by which we
enter into the rhythm of life that God designed.

For all of us, particularly activists and advocates of justice,
sabbath rest is important. According to Daniel Hill, activists often
have a sense that "if they don't push this rock, shake this tree, declare the truth," then change will not occur. A danger of living as an
activist is "thinking we are God." Sabbath forces us to remember
that we are *not* God. We need to know that, as Hill says, "The world
is going to be okay if we take a day off." God cares about issues of
justice far more than we do. Whatever we are doing, God desires to

use us; but he doesn't need us to accomplish his purposes.

Another reason sabbath rest is critical for activists is that the work is so terribly hard. Hill doesn't pull any punches: "We are fools if we think we can work day in and day out without having physical rest." What good is it if we go hard for three years and then burn out? Shouldn't we instead work diligently and practice healthy rhythms so that we can stay in the game for the long haul? The longer we are able to stay in the game, the more potential we have to help effect long-term changes.

The challenges of our faith are not only internal struggles or battles against earthly injustice. Rather, we are fighting against real spiritual evil: "Injustice is the manifestation of the evil one," Hill says. Systematic injustices are more than social inequality; they are also spiritual death traps, which are deeply connected to spiritual warfare in the heavenly realms. Hill states: "We should never take lightly how serious . . . the things are we fight against." If we are going to be successful working against spiritual oppression and global injustice, we must be intimately connected with God. Sabbath "reconnects us with God and gives us a heavenly vision to provoke change without seeing the unseen." The global justice movement, apart from connection with God, won't change social, systemic or spiritual evils. Thus, Christians must observe the sabbath in order to be sustained and to stay in tune with the work and direction of the Spirit of God.

CONTEMPORARY PRAXIS

Regardless of one's call or vocation, Christians can intentionally create space for worship, reflection, rest and sabbath. These are particularly important practices for people working in ministries of mercy and justice and people who are passionately driven to bring about change in the world. Sometimes the driving factors are healthy. Other times, for good or bad, personal reasons motivate activists. These reasons may surface from personal history and the psyches of individuals. Understanding the source of one's energy to bring about change is valuable work. On one hand, Christ-followers are God's hands and feet in the world. On the other, God does not need us to accomplish his will and purposes. For activists, rest may not be as high a value as the desire to bring about change. The importance of the task at hand can sometimes limit a person's ability to find balance and rhythm regarding sleep, rest, self-care and observation of the sabbath.

Throughout the Bible, writers place emphasis on healthy rhythm and the observance of the sabbath as a way to honor God and rest from the toils of one's labor. Looking at Bishop Tutu's example, one becomes deeply convicted about the necessity of observing the sabbath as a meaningful spiritual practice that enhances efforts and movements of justice. Rest for the body and rest for the soul are necessary components of a healthy Christian life. The more we are able to rest our bodies and nourish our souls, the more effective we will be advocating for justice and change in the world.

Christians engage in faith practices as antidotes for weariness. When we take the time to intentionally meet with God and to rest from "doing," we allow ourselves to enter into the process of "being" with our Lord and Creator. Several of the faith practices introduced so far—silence, prayer, worship and study—are excellent ways to intentionally rest in the presence of God. These activities shouldn't be pursued as a means of "accomplishing" something, but rather out of a love for God and the opportunity to fellowship with him. God put sabbath rhythms into place so that all people and creation might have the opportunity for replenishment and revitalization. Sabbath allows followers of Christ to have a glimpse of God's peace and shalom in this world while praying that God's will would be done on earth as it is in heaven.

◆ Rule of Life

In *The Life You've Always Wanted,* John Ortberg includes an exercise to help people develop their own "rule of life," by which every activity of the day is submitted to the name of Jesus. He instructs his readers to consider what it would mean to do every day-to-day activity in "the way Jesus himself would": waking up, greeting your family, eating, driving, working, caring for children, shopping, watching television, doing household tasks or whatever else your day might hold. He says, "Keep it simple. Focus on Jesus' presence with you as you go through these seemingly inconsequential moments of the day. Keep directing your thoughts back to him."[36] Do you have activities in your life that allow you to be close to God, that create space for you to develop relationships with others and that address injustices in your surrounding community? This may seem like a very simple way to start, but submitting different components of our day to God is a way of reconnecting with him.

◆ Sleep

Helen Cepero, professor of spiritual formation at North Park Theological Seminary, reminds her students that sleep is a "soul training" exercise and a spiritual practice.[37] In James Bryan Smith's book *The Good and Beautiful God: Falling in Love with the God Jesus Knows,* he describes spiritual formation as a combination of "our action and God's action."[38] Smith makes a powerful case "that sleep is integral to spiritual formation because if our bodies suffer, our souls suffer as well."[39] Cepero claims that sleep teaches us about ourselves and about God.[40] According to Smith, "Sleep is an act of surrender. It is a declaration of trust. It is admitting that we are not God (who never sleeps), and that is good news."[41]

The biblical story of Elijah is a good example of the necessity of sleep. After feeling deserted and believing that he was "the only one of the Lord's prophets left" (1 Kings 18:22), Elijah fled to the wilderness. After having traveled a few days journey into the wilderness, Elijah came to a broom bush, sat down under it and "prayed that he might die" (1 Kings 19:4). Feeling sorry for himself, Elijah was depleted physically and emotionally. He had given up on life. He prayed to God, "Take my life" (1 Kings 19:4), and then he went to sleep. The Lord sent an angel, who woke up Elijah and gave him food and drink. After being nourished, Elijah lay back down again and slept more. The story continues that after Elijah had rested both body and soul, he went and stood on the mountain. There the Lord revealed his presence (1 Kings 19:10-13). Elijah's plight is a good reminder that even those most loyal and anointed to do the work of God need rest and nourishment for their bodies and spirits. It was only after Elijah had rested and received the nourishment of food and drink that he was able to hear the word of God.

◆ *Observation of the Sabbath*

Observation of the sabbath does not have to happen on a Sunday. The day of the week for practicing rest is not the most important issue. For pastors, Sunday is often a work day, and while corporate worship may nourish their souls, Sundays typically do not include much physical rest. It is helpful, if possible, to observe the same day of the week regularly. This allows you to develop a rhythm as you enter into rest.

One might ask what types of things you should do in order to observe the sabbath. Consider what types of activities (or lack thereof!) are recreational and which ones that you enjoy. Perhaps reading a book, watching a movie or talking a walk is refreshing for you. When I was in college, sabbath meant taking one day off from studying. Every Sunday I would treat myself to "rest" by going to church in the morning and then spending the afternoon at home reading a good book. I much looked forward to Sundays!

You might also ask what types of activities make you feel connected to God. Perhaps reading the Bible, listening to worship music or writing in your journal nourishes your soul. Tutu reminds us: "Being made for God means, for us, that anything less than God will not suffice. We are hungry for God, but we don't always know that it is God that we crave."[42] The idea is not to be legalistic but to provide the opportunity to connect with God and experience rest.

◆ *Sabbatical*

Similar principles are at play in the observation of the sabbath and in the spiritual practice of taking a sabbatical. Sabbaticals are a version of sabbath rest and are based on the same Hebrew word *shabbat.* Sabbaticals typically refer to rest for more extensive periods of time. For example, many churches encourage their pastoral staff to take a few months of rest every seven years of service. Some parts of the corporate world have acknowledged the benefits of allowing their employees to take sabbaticals after an appropriate length of service. In 2011, hundreds of workplaces around the United States included sabbaticals in order to "attract, retain, and accelerate top talent through personal and professional enrichment."[43] For example, American Express allotted up to twenty-four weeks of sabbatical time for certain employees with a given length of service. Similarly, eBay offers their employees up to four weeks for a sabbatical. Procter & Gamble offers up to twelve weeks away. Taking a sabbatical provides a long period of rest, nourishment and reflection.

It would be naïve to think that sabbaticals are a viable option for everyone in today's society. A sabbatical rest offered by a church or corporation is a significant privilege, and one that allows time and space without the burden of worrying about income and financial constraints. Sabbaticals are particularly necessary for people who are engaged in lots of activity and are "doers," such as activists and advocates.

◆ *Retreat*

Retreating is a valuable way to set aside time for rest and reflection in the presence of God. Many churches offer family retreats or retreats targeted to men and women who are a part of the church community. Retreats may only last for a few days but provide the opportunity to step out of the daily challenges of life for the purpose of recreation, rest and spiritual reflection. Retreats can also focus us on God's heart for the world. Retreats can be a wonderful way of gaining perspective and nourishing one's soul.

I once heard a Christian leader complain that pastors at his church were "retreating" all of the time. In other words, he thought that there was too much rest and lack of activity by the church's pastoral staff. This Christian leader had a fair point. Pastors and church staff should diligently apply themselves to their work through the practice of a good work ethic, doing their best and investing time and energy into the ministries of the church. Still, there are very legitimate reasons to retreat, rest and spend intentional time apart from the work of ministry in order to be in the presence of God. Even leaders like Martin Luther King Jr. recognized the need for rest and reflection. King said, "What I have been doing is giving, giving, giving and not stopping to retreat and meditate like I should—to come back. If the situation is not changed, I will be a physical and psychological wreck, I have to reorganize my personality and reorient my life."[44]

7

Oscar Romero

FROM SUBMISSION TO MARTYRDOM

Submit to one another out of reverence for Christ.

EPHESIANS 5:21

As A PART OF MY MINISTRY responsibilities at Willow Creek, I led the local and national groups involved in prison ministry. The leadership team told me repeatedly about a prison in rural Louisiana. The prison, Louisiana State Penitentiary at Angola, had a reputation during the middle of the twentieth century as being the "bloodiest prison" in America. In recent years, however, a new warden had taken over. Burl Cain is known for his strict, no-nonsense methodologies and his devout faith in God. Cain became the warden of Angola in 1995. His tenure began a remarkable transformation within the prison which honored the dignity and respect of the incarcerated men while also demanding constructive engagement and positive contributions. I first went to Angola in 2006.

During my visit, I spent a day with several inmates who were a part of the seminary program. Some of the changes Warden Cain had brought to the prison included religious reforms and the opportunity for inmates to participate in church services and community. My team and I looked forward to engaging with the seminarians in prison, almost all of whom had "trustee" status for good behavior and who were serving life sentences. After I introduced our team, I said that we would be spending the next few hours together talking about spiritual disciplines. Since our time was very limited, I asked the men which disciplines they struggled with the most and how they wanted us to focus. Without hesitation, they responded in unity. The two primary disciplines they struggled with were *solitude* and *submission*.

The identification of these two disciplines as the most difficult to practice in the prison setting makes sense. The inmates live in dormitories and rarely, if ever, are unaccompanied by a guard or someone else. Solitude, the physical aspect of being alone, is nearly impossible. Submission is similarly difficult. The inmates are required by law and circumstance to submit. They don't have much choice. They wake up when it is demanded of them. They gather in line for "count" several times a day. They go where they are supposed to go. What does submission look like in circumstances where so little is under one's control?

We spent a couple of hours looking through the Scriptures and seeking to better understand God's heart in regard to both solitude and submission. As the day came to a close, we decided that we would attempt to practice the things we had been learning. While the challenges of the inmates to practice the disciplines of solitude and submission were real, we still believed there was opportunity for spiritual engagement. Together we entered into a time of prayer and quiet. Our hope was to create a sense of solitude in a room full of people. One of the people present opened our time in prayer. We put on a CD which had some quiet worship music to help fill the space with contemplative reminders that God was present with us. There were different stations around the room where people could go to sit and pray, journal or otherwise reflect on the presence of God.

After about thirty minutes, we invited the seminarians to enter into an exercise of submission. Our final station was set up outside the doors of the room where we had been meeting. As the inmates came out of the room, they were invited to have their feet washed by our team.

One might ask how foot washing is an exercise of submission. Submission may be defined as the process of yielding power or authority to another or as being subjected to some kind of treatment or influence.[1] Foot washing exemplifies submission in several ways. As someone washes another person's feet, that person is yielding power by showing respect and authority for the recipient of the act. During the New Testament era, foot washing was a tradition of hospitality typically performed by a slave or a servant for special guests and those visiting a home. How radical it must have been for the disciples to see Jesus prepare to wash their feet. No wonder Peter was so reluctant! Yet Jesus responded to Peter, "Unless I wash you, you have no part with me" (Jn 13:8). As Jesus washed the feet of his disciples, he was entering into a physical posture of submission. He took the position of a slave, modeling humility and service. The disciples, however, in the act of receiving Christ's service, also submitted. They were subjected to the service of Christ's actions. At first, Peter was unwilling. As he heard the corrective words of Jesus, Peter responded emphatically, "Then, Lord . . . not just my feet but my hands and my head as well!" (Jn 13:9).

In Angola that day, several of us sat on the floor. One by one, we washed the feet of the inmates who were willing. As we washed, we prayed over them. As we prayed, the Spirit of God moved powerfully. Several of us, both our team and the inmates, were overcome by tears as we entered into the act of submission together. In this ritual, we submitted to one another through an act of service and the act of receiving. Regardless of our circumstances, we all have small choices of submission to God and to one another. I learned a great deal that day from my friends in Angola. They regularly teach me about what it means to be faithful to the call of Christ under challenging circumstances.

OSCAR ROMERO

As I considered who would be an appropriate model of the spiritual practice of submission, Oscar Romero immediately came to mind. Oscar Arnulfo Romero was a twentieth-century Roman Catholic archbishop who worked tirelessly for social justice and in defense of human rights.[2]

Romero was born on August 15, 1917, in Ciudad Barrios, a small town in El Salvador.[3] From a very young age, Romero wanted to be a priest. At fourteen years old, he headed to San Miguel, where he could attend school and pursue his vocation. At the age of twenty, Romero went to the national Jesuit seminary in San Salvador.[4] He eventually attended the Gregorian Pontifical University in Rome and in 1943 received his degree in theology.[5] At twenty-four years old, Romero was ordained in Rome.[6] After ordination into priesthood, he returned to San Salvador, where he began his vocational ministry and served as a parish priest in a small community called Anamoros. Soon thereafter, he was appointed to the position of the diocesan secretary in San Miguel, where he served in different capacities for twenty-three years.[7] In 1967, Romero became known as "Monseñor" and was named the secretary general of Salvadoran Bishops' Conference. For the remainder of his life, his primary residence would be the capital city of San Salvador. In 1970, Romero received his Episcopal ordination as auxiliary bishop.[8] Up until this point in his life, Romero was known for his fairness and honesty and his overt support of the Catholic Church and the wealthy individuals who supported it.

From the early years of his ministry, in spite of his allegiance to the church and its supporters, Romero was also known for his genuine concern for the poor. He was politically and theologically conservative, which explained some of his allegiances to organizations and people in authority. Romero was a friend of the government and of the rich landowners, many of whom were coffee growers.[9] As divisions between the rich and poor in El Salvador increased, Romero preached good news for the poor and sought to draw them closer to God while at the same time preaching a message of salvation to the rich and encouraging them to draw closer to the poor. He was influenced by the birth of liberation theology, which burst onto the scene in Latin America in the mid-1960s.[i] Although he didn't adhere to the theology personally, he paid close attention to others who were involved in the movement. Around the same, in 1968, the Conference of Latin American Bishops gathered in Medellín, Colombia, as a part of the global response to the Second Vatican Council (1962-65). Romero was present at the Medellín meetings and was very influenced by the Pope's statement regarding "Evangelism in the Modern World."[10] In 1977, as El Salvador was in the grip of social and political repression, Oscar Romero became archbishop of San Salvador.[11]

TWENTIETH-CENTURY EL SALVADOR

Romero's home country was a place of turmoil throughout the late nineteenth and twentieth centuries. After coffee-growing was introduced in 1828, peasants were thoroughly exploited and their pay was derisory. El Salvador increasingly became a police state, and respect for human rights was almost nonexistent. Many trace the seeds of violence to 1932, when military dictators took over

---

[i]Liberation theology, with streams founded by Gustavo Gutierrez and James Cone, emphasizes Christ's death on the cross as a source of liberation for people who are disinherited and suffer oppression.

after killing almost thirty thousand people and crushing a communist-inspired peasant uprising.[12] An impoverished, suffering population longed for relief, but anyone who said anything about justice was thrown into prison or killed. In this context, Romero grew up desiring to become a priest in order to provide comfort and care to the people of El Salvador.[13]

In the 1930s, when Romero was still a student, the Roman Catholic Church aligned with the military and wealthy coffee-plantation owners. By the 1960s, there was a widening gap between the rich and the poor and increased military oppression.[14] Formally, the Catholic Church continued to support those in power, while individual parish priests often sided with the people most affected by unjust policies. Many clergy were conflicted about the growing intensity of oppression. Romero empathized with the poor but did not overtly challenge the wealthy. He taught about God's love but did not directly address the growing injustice. By the 1970s, the tumult was continuing to escalate.

On July 30, 1975, forty university students were killed by the Salvadoran military in San Salvador. Many priests and religious people joined the student protest movement when they occupied the cathedral in San Salvador. Romero, however, criticized "the occupation of churches as a form of protest."[15] For Romero, 1976 marked a year full of events that would begin to shift his perspective and allegiance from the militaristic government and land-holding elites to those suffering at their hands. He returned to work directly with the people as the bishop of Santiago de María. His ideological convictions and theological underpinnings began to shift. Romero was particularly troubled by the massacre of five peasants in his diocesan village of Tres Calles at the hands of the Salvadoran National Guard.[16] By 1977, according to a biographer of Romero's, the bishops in El Salvador "expressed their concern for the violence against the peasants, for the deaths and disappearances, for the publicity campaign, threats, and intimidation against the church, and for the expulsion of priests in particular."[17] The lack of social justice and the overt state of suffering for many Salvadorans was intense. El Salvador was ridden with overt human rights abuses directed at the poor and at those in the church who tried to protect them.

On February 20, 1977, Romero was installed as archbishop. He was considered a safe choice because of his allegiance to the wealthy and to the government. Only a few weeks after his installation, his perspective on the coffee growers and the military began to shift drastically.

ROMERO'S CONVERSION AT THE DEATH OF FATHER RIO GRANDE

Father Rutilio Grande was a Jesuit priest and close friend of Bishop Romero. Grande had been an outspoken defender of the rights of the poor and, in the words of Scott Wright, a leader in the Jesuit mission of "the proclamation of faith and the defense of justice."[18] Around this time, the landowners engaged in a countermovement to continue the repression of the poor. A right-wing death squad appeared on the scene and messages of "Be a patriot: kill a priest" were announced on radios and appeared in newspapers.[19] As tensions escalated, the right-wing military and wealthy elite increased their mechanisms of terror to squelch any opposition to their dominance and control. On March 13, 1977, Rutilio Grande was on his way to Aguilares, the community where he had been a pastor, to perform an evening mass, when he, an elderly man and a boy were shot and killed in an ambush.[20]

Many biographers argue that the murder of Father Grande, Romero's dear friend, was the watershed moment for the shift in Romero's convictions.[21] After Grande's death, Romero's message and response to the church's partnership with the powerful and elite waned. Throughout his life, Romero was loyal to the church. When he witnessed the death of his dear friend and the traumas enacted upon the poor throughout El Salvador, however, Romero didn't hesitate to be a prophetic voice declaring injustice. He proclaimed in one of his sermons: "[The church] is not to be measured by the government's support but rather by its own authenticity." As government soldiers tortured and executed innocent people, Romero boldly stated, "Like a voice crying in the wilderness, we must continually say no to violence and yes to peace."

Romero made a controversial and bold decision after Grande's death. He chose to have one singular mass for the region and to close the Catholic schools for three days in protest of the death of Father Rutilio Grande.[22] At a liturgy celebrated in front of the cathedral, 100,000 people gathered and the Archbishop condemned the actions of El Salvador's leaders. He called on government officials to exercise human rights and stop committing crimes of injustice toward the population.[23] This was seen as an overt statement against the dictatorial regime and those perpetrating the violence against the peasants. Romero's response to Grande's assassination sounded an alarm at the Vatican.[24] From that time forward, Romero became the leading voice for the end of violence and oppression to the poor. He preached and used his influential position as archbishop to stand up against the gross injustices occurring throughout El Salvador.

Presiding over Grande's funeral, Romero began to incarnate his theological understanding of submission. Some say the spirit of Father Grande and his concern for the gross injustice against the poor was transferred to Romero in his death. One biographer wrote: "One martyr gave life to another martyr. Before the cadaver of Father Rutilio Grande, Monseñor Romero, in his twentieth day of archbishop, felt the call of Christ to overcome his natural human timidity and to be filled with the fortitude of an apostle."[25] At the funeral, the archbishop preached a sermon on John 15:13: "Greater love has no one than this: to lay down one's life for one's friends." The sacrifice of one's life, for Romero, was the ultimate act of submission.[26] Romero taught that the church must be inspired by faith, engaged in the struggle for liberation of the poor and motivated by love.[27]

On May 11, 1977, a few months after Grande's murder, another priest, Father Alfonso Navarro, was assassinated. Romero spoke of Navarro's message to reject violence: "They kill me because I point the way to follow. And we, the church, repeat once more that violence resolves nothing, violence is not Christian, not human."[28] Romero continued to preach love and care for the poor with an emphasis on evangelization. He taught about God's concern for justice and against the persecution of the church as the "light of the Gospel."[29] He also continued to view the harsh conditions in El Salvador with a perspective of hope and encouragement. He believed persecution against priests was a sign of God's presence and favor. He preached: "Today in his Gospel [Luke 9:18-24] Jesus told us that those who wish to come after him must deny themselves, take up their cross, and follow."[30] Suffering, even to the point of martyrdom, was a part of taking up the cross of Christ. Romero believed: "Christians who live out their baptism become saints and heroes."[31] By 1979, Romero's work on behalf of the poor in El Salvador led to his nomination for the Nobel Peace Prize. That year, Mother Teresa received the prestigious award.

SOURCE OF POWER AND CONVICTION

Oscar Romero practiced Ignatian spiritual exercises.[32] He believed in the power of prayer and sought to submit himself fully before God.[33] In 1955, Romero spent a month engaging in the spiritual exercises of St. Ignatius of Loyola under the spiritual direction of Miguel Elizondo. He found the exercises deeply meaningful and spent several hours a day in prayer and an hour or so conferring with his spiritual director. He wrote of the experience: "The material offered for meditation and prayer is designed to lead to a more generous following of Christ, who invites the person to help extend his reign through service in the church."[34] These exercises and his direct connection to God played, as one biographer put it, "a fundamental force in his life."[35]

Romero believed that Christ is not distant from human suffering but that he manifests himself as Emmanuel—God with us—in the midst of the challenging political circumstances of the day. Romero believed that followers of Christ must embrace suffering. In 1980, he preached that people should pray not to be delivered from pain and suffering but rather to "embrace it."[36]

Romero called people to live in community and to depend on one another.[37] Faith is not separate from the daily reality of their lives. Romero called people to pious devotion and commitment in the midst of their circumstances. He exhorted: "All practices that disagree with the gospel must be removed if we are to save people. We must save not the soul at the hour of death but the person living in history."[38]

PREFERENTIAL OPTION FOR THE POOR

Oscar Romero emphasized God's preferential option for the poor. He believed the lives of the priests who had been killed underscored this truth. In presiding over Holy Communion, he shared these words: "When I celebrate the Eucharist with you, I feel them present. Each priest killed is for me a new concelebrant in the Eucharist of our archdiocese. I know that they are here giving us encouragement by having known how to die without fear, because each one's conscience was committed to this law of the Lord: the preferential option for the poor."[39]

Romero called the church to solidarity with the poor. He identified the effects of poverty in El Salvador as the fate of the poor "to

be taken away, to be tortured, to be jailed, to be found dead."[40] Increasingly, Romero's ministry became characterized by his solidarity with those who suffered. He traveled the countryside
meeting the brokenhearted and visiting garbage dumps to comfort
the suffering and reclaim the dead.[41] In 1979 he preached: "My
position as pastor obliges me to solidarity with everyone who
suffers and to embody every effort for human freedom and
dignity."[42]

Romero had a rich theological interpretation of poverty. He
viewed poverty as the Christian spirit of openness to God. He believed "the poorer you are, the more you possess God's kingdom."[43]
He highly valued the words of Jesus in the Sermon on the Mount,
"Blessed are the poor in spirit, for theirs is the kingdom of heaven"
(Mt 5:3). Poverty, for Romero, "awakens consciousness" and leads
people to be more open to the kingdom and presence of God.
Romero lived his life among the poor. He resolved that he would
do whatever it was that the Lord asked. Increasingly, his life exemplified a spirit of submission to speak truth boldly to those in
power. Romero resolved to be faithful even in the midst of hor-
rendous violence.

AGAINST INJUSTICE AND CORRUPTION

Bishop Romero not only argued for solidarity in suffering with the
poor. He also overtly stood up against injustice. He spoke boldly
against the powers of his day. The world does not welcome a
prophet. The powers that practice injustice do not welcome re-
proach or correction, and they resist a call to conversion. They respond with violence and increased fervor. Romero never gave up
on calling the unjust to conversion. He boldly invited them to repentance: "I cry out against injustice, but only to say to the unjust:
Be converted! I cry out in the name of suffering, of those who
suffer injustice, but only to say to the criminals: Be converted! Do

not be wicked!"[44] He spoke to them with love and accepted their hatred as a part of his cross. Romero loved his enemies while attempting to lead them to an alternative way of life. He prayed for them and called his enemies to conversion: "Therefore, dear brothers and sisters, especially those of you who hate me, you dear brothers and sisters who think I am preaching violence, who defame me and know it isn't true, you that have hands stained with murder, with torture, with atrocity, with injustice—be converted. I love you deeply. I am sorry for you because you go on the way to ruin."[45]

All the while, Romero desired for the perpetrators of violence to be drawn to Christ. Romero accompanied the poor in their suffering and directly confronted the powers that oppressed them.

ULTIMATE ACT OF SUBMISSION

Romero's life exemplified Romans 12:1: "I urge you, brothers and sisters, in view of God's mercy, to offer your bodies as a living sacrifice, holy and pleasing to God—this is your true and proper worship." Romero was willing to offer his position, power, influence and life for the sake of those who suffered. He regularly thought and preached about God's call to submission. He considered Romans 12 an opportunity for all people, regardless of status or position: "Here, you see, the Bible gives our bodies, our lives, a meaning of sacrifice, of holocaust, a divine meaning that is proper to every person, even the lowliest."[46] The opportunity to sacrifice and suffer alongside of others gave life meaning and purpose.

Romero opposed all types of violence except that which allowed one to suffer for the sake of someone else. In 1979 Romero preached about the violence of love that occurred on the cross: "The only violence that the gospel admits is violence to oneself. When Christ lets himself be killed, that is violence—letting oneself be killed. Violence to oneself is more effective than violence to others. It is very easy to kill, especially when one has weapons, but how hard it is to let oneself be killed for love of the people!"[47]

Increasingly, Romero spoke out boldly in opposition to the rampant murders throughout El Salvador. He used his position as archbishop to call attention to the suffering of his people. Romero did not fear the consequences of his own suffering. He once said, "I must tell you, as a Christian, I do not believe in death without resurrection. If I am killed, I shall arise in the Salvadoran people."[48] He openly criticized his country's military for its role in the violence and murder. He cried out against them: "In the name of God, and in the name of this suffering people whose laments rise to heaven each day . . . I beg you, I ask you, I order you in the name of God: Stop the repression!"[49]

On March 24, 1980, Romero was conducting mass and had just finished giving the homily. He was speaking these words:

> This holy mass, this Eucharist, is an act of faith. With Christian faith we know that at this moment the wheaten host is changed into the body of the Lord, who offered himself for the world's redemption, and in this chalice the wine is transformed into the blood that was the price of salvation. May this body immolated and this blood sacrificed for humans nourish us also, so that we may give our body and blood to suffering and to pain—like Christ, not for self, but to teach justice and peace to our people.[50]

At that moment, a shot rang out from the back of the church. Romero was shot in the chest. Blood covered his vestments and he gasped for breath. He died moments later.[51]

ROMERO'S LEGACY

The funeral of Oscar Romero was itself an occasion of further violence. As thousands gathered to pay their respects to the archbishop of San Salvador, the military and police fired shots into the crowds of people who had gathered. In addition to those who were killed by the gunfire, others died as they were trampled by the crowd of people trying to take refuge in the cathedral.[52] The situation in El Salvador got far worse before things began to improve. While workers, peasants, students and teachers organized in massive grassroots organizations, the nation teetered on the edge of civil war. The government responded by increasing violence and oppression. In 1980, the year of Romero's assassination, more than twelve thousand people were killed.[53] El Salvador entered into twelve years of overt war between 1980 and 1992, with a litany of suffering that included more than 1.5 million people forced into exile, 7,000 disappearances and 75,000 deaths.[54] According to the U.N. Truth Commission, the Salvadoran government and the death squads accounted for the vast majority of these deaths.[55]

Oscar Romero's life and death are examples of ultimate submission. He embraced his call to serve the church and God's people even unto death. While directly confronting injustice, he suggested that one should never tire of teaching love, for it is a force that will "overcome the world." [56] The violence of love was the only type of violence he promoted. He stood up to the institutions of the church and the oppressive militaristic regime of El Salvador. Empowered by God and working with the poor in the name of Christ, he stood tall against the brutal death brigades funded by the wealthy and elite. Romero's submission to Christ bears witness to life. Just as Christ was resurrected on the third day, Romero, as he promised, has been resurrected in the lives of the Salvadoran people.

ALEXIA SALVATIERRA: NO MATTER WHAT THE COST

I first met Alexia Salvatierra a few years ago at a gathering in Washington, D.C., that focused on domestic poverty and called lawmakers to address the devastating effects of poverty in the United States. I was familiar with Salvatierra's reputation as one of the most effective grassroots organizers in the country. She is an Evangelical Lutheran pastor and the executive director of Clergy and Laity United for Economic Justice (CLUE), an organization of religious leaders in southern California who support low-wage workers in their struggle for a living wage, health insurance, fair working conditions and a voice in the decisions that affect them. She has committed her life to discrediting the "great lie" that some people are worth more than others.[57]

Even knowing her reputation, however, I was unprepared for the passion and vitality Alexia embodies. She is one of the most committed and fervent people I know. She radiates love and acceptance with an accompanying tidal wave of conviction about overcoming the injustices that affect people daily. Her love for God and her heart for people in poverty overwhelm those who encounter her. When I spoke with Alexia about her ministry, she reminded me that "being a spiritual giant is not necessarily what the spiritual life is all about." Rather, she said, our spiritual lives should be "more about God and less about us."[58] The greatest gift for Alexia is to be "called to battle on the side of your Lord." She describes following Christ as both harsh and beautiful. It is as if Christ is a general riding on horseback. Jesus turns around and says "Are you ready?" Her response: "Yes, my Lord."

Alexia could tell many stories of ways she has seen God move through grassroots organizing campaigns. One story includes the CEO of one of America's largest and most influential retail corporations. Alexia was advocating for seventy thousand employees of the company with regard to health care. Someone else involved in the campaign for health care had learned that the CEO was a Christian. The campaign organizers, including Alexia, decided that they would like to reach out to the CEOs pastor, to explain the way the company's policies caused suffering among several thousand employees and to see whether the pastor could encourage the CEO to reconsider his policies. But they didn't know where the CEO went to church, nor how to contact his pastor.

One day, Reverend Salvatierra was preaching a sermon in a church several hundred miles away from where the corporation was based. She included mention of the health care crisis and how it would affect the workers. After the service, a young woman came forward and told Salvatierra that her father was an elder at the church where the CEO attended. The woman had never attended the church before and just happened to be there on the particular Sunday that Salvatierra preached. Now, having identified the church through this woman, Salvatierra and other campaign leaders were able to reach out to the pastor and lead a peaceful prayer movement, which touched the heart of the CEO. The end result: the corporation's policies changed to reflect more fair treatment of the workers. The crisis was averted. This case was a dramatic one in which God intervened powerfully.

Alexia Salvatierra identified three very different "ways of faith" in her own personal engagement: hope, nonviolence and humility. The first "way of faith" is embodied in hope. Alexia described hope as a means of "illuminating victory." The fight against injustice can often seem impossible to win. But because of the power of the resurrection, what might otherwise seem impossible can become "improbable," indicating a margin of possibility for change to occur. "The victory is not necessarily a simple and clear destination," Alexia says. "There is a mystery in it, but there is also the promise of victory." Alexia described this hope as a sustaining power in her own work and ministry. Often struggles against injustice involve huge differentials in power. The oppressed have little opportunity and few material resources to use in their struggle. Hope recalibrates this power difference and enables those in the struggle to see possibilities for change.

Salvatierra and the communities she works alongside have

fought many battles that everyone else said would be impossible. One such example is her advocacy with workers in the hotel industry. This particular campaign included CLUE and several partner organizations, such as HERE Local 11 and the Los Angeles Alliance for a New Economy. In previous times, hotel owners usually lived in area where their hotels were located. Owners had a stake in the community, and it was possible for organizers to talk with them directly when there were concerns about unfair treatment. Increasingly, however, huge conglomerates have taken over the hotel industry, and people in leadership no longer have connections with the local community.

The workers in this particular community realized they needed a national voice so that they could stand together as a unified coalition to talk to the owners. Each hotel conglomerate, however, had different timelines and years for their employee contracts. For example, employee representatives from the Hyatt in New York and the Hyatt in Los Angeles couldn't go to the negotiating table at the same time because their contracts had different years. So CLUE and their partner organizations targeted five cities in which they would ask hotels to line up their contracts in the same year. They targeted a goal of new contracts that would last for two to three years. At the start of the campaign, the alignment seemed completely impossible. Why would the companies ever agree to align their contracts? From a financial perspective, it would not be to their advantage.

Led by immigrants and housekeepers from all over the world, a movement began in Los Angeles. The women who gathered had a deep faith in God. Many were single mothers and the only ones who provided for their families. These women often cleaned sixteen hotel rooms a day and went home to hungry children who were not insured through their full-time employment in the hotel industry. These women mobilized a movement to stand up to the hotel owners and to bring change. As Salvatierra told the story, she described a picture reminiscent of the small shepherd boy, David, standing tall to the Philistine giant, Goliath. In their own strength, these women and mothers did not have the ability to change their circumstances. They asked clergy and others from the interfaith community to walk with them in their struggle. They leaned heavily on their profound faith in God. Salvatierra says, "God really walks with these women . . . there is no question about it." Prayer significantly contributed to the efforts of these women to bring about change. Still, the struggle seemed impossible.

The women workers led the movement, while pastors and church leaders of different faiths supported them. In one very big hotel in downtown Los Angeles, a Methodist bishop stood outside of the hotel to preach. She had been struck by how many times she had stayed in hotels and been cared for over her lifetime. She said to the hotel workers, "You have taken care of me. Now I want to take care of you." She advocated for them to have a living wage and insurance to be able to provide for their children. Quietly, faith leaders walked through the hotels—into the pools, bars and restaurants—to raise awareness with patrons about the conditions of workers in the hotels. After the clergy were set up in their locations, they began to preach with the hopes of changing the hotel owners' hearts. They preached about God's heart for love and justice. They told stories about what was happening in the lives of women who were working in the hotels.

The campaign had expected that the clergy would be kicked out immediately and that they would then tell their story to the press. But once the clergy began preaching, the hotel management didn't know what to do about it. They didn't want to interfere. Instead of being kicked out, the clergy preached. They told their stories. People listened.

Alexia described aspects of this event as a "great evangelical experience." God was laughing. Eventually, the faith leaders were indeed kicked out of the hotels and were able to tell their story to the press. The religious leaders not only told of the condition of the workers in the hotel, but some also shared about Christ. They shared the story of his suffering and the hope that faith in him provides. They related Christ to people in everyday life. That day in the campaign was a great moment of triumph. After about a year of walking alongside of the workers, the campaign was successful. Against all odds, they won! The workers got their contracts aligned so they could negotiate with other workers across the country at the same time. By God's grace and their efforts, they changed their working conditions, which had once been so unjust. Salvatierra describes the campaign as an amazing experience. "Never once did those women doubt that we would win," she says. Their faith gave them confidence to persevere when earthly circumstances seemed dim. This story exemplifies the "way of faith" Salvatierra embodies when she talks about hope in the impossible.

The second "way of faith" Salvatierra describes is the way of nonviolence. "Nonviolence as a way to the cross is not natural to me," she says. "Passion is natural to me." Nonviolence is a discipline of submission. Salvatierra looks to Jesus as a model for nonviolent activism in the world and sees his model as the better way. In describing the difference between her natural inclinations and the way of the cross, she says, "I possess the willingness to follow the goal, regardless of the cost. But nonviolence is not natural to me. Jesus unites power and love that are not united in the world. I tend to be a ruthless person. Jesus is not ruthless." Rather, Jesus modeled a way of combating injustice that was full of love. He was direct and powerful. He was also nonviolent.

The way for justice workers to tap into this power of nonviolence is through intimate connection with God. As we allow ourselves to die and take up the mantle of the cross, our human nature is overcome by the nature of God. Alexia describes this process in her own life: "I need to rest in him. Resting. Resting is necessary." As she rests in God, she is able to embrace nonviolence as a means of provoking change. Romero similarly went through this process of transformation. After the death of Father Grande, Romero had a conversion experience, in which he came to see injustice more directly than ever before. In his response, he rested in God and became a changed man. Salvatierra describes this transformation: "Romero had to travel a very long way in his own consciousness to do what he did. He came from privilege. He was conservative. He did not break the rules. But he was broken by Jesus. The Lord took him somewhere . . . somewhere he would never have gone alone." Ultimately, Romero gave up his life as he embraced of nonviolence as a means for combating injustice.

The third "way of faith" for Reverend Salvatierra is humility. Sanctification requires acknowledging our brokenness and that of humanity and discovering that we are still loved. The reality of God's love for us is paradoxical. Similarly, Salvatierra describes the process of creating justice as a "paradoxical process." As one becomes increasingly aware that she is shattered, broken and disconnected, she must pursue justice differently. One can't stay angry all of the time when one encounters injustice, because there is a greater understanding of one's own human frailty and sin. All of us, in some way, shape or form, contribute to injustice at different points in our lives. Regardless of our frailty, justice is pursued by turning everything over to Jesus in a spirit of submission and constant prayer.

For Alexia Salvatierra, this dependence on God has never failed: "I have a very living relationship with Jesus who is with me all of the time." Alexia also works. Constantly. As she works, she communes with God. "If I am not preaching on a Sunday morning, I am out working." Her work is intimately connected to her relationship with God. She tells of this interconnection exemplified in the sacrament of Communion: "As a Lutheran pastor, Communion is very important to me." Some of her favorite memories of celebrating the Eucharist are from her college days at the University of California, Santa Cruz, when she and a group of friends would gather before dawn to share Holy Communion at sunrise. She describes the experience: "We would take bread and wine and celebrate Communion with God." Alexia deeply connects to God through her work for justice. As she seeks to make the world right, she is empowered by her relationship and connection with God.

Salvatierra's own life story models the humility she esteems so highly. She has committed herself to following God "no matter what the cost." Salvatierra describes herself as someone who is "not always good about following the rules." She runs on the "impulse to do wild things for God" and relentlessly pushes forth: "When I see the goal, I don't care about the cost and will do what God calls me to do." She says, "I am not sure that it is a mark of spiritual maturity but a mark of personality that God utilizes." God takes her to unexpected places. He uses her faithfulness to provoke and facilitate change when change seems impossible. Salvatierra has willingly entered into the suffering of people who are hurting for the sake of Christ. She says, "I have always felt the pain of other people in my own body as if it were mine. I always felt the need to do something when people were hurting. Jesus gave me the hope that it could be done. Before I was in Jesus, the world looked too dark for me. Jesus gave me the hope that justice was possible." Thus, this vibrant woman of God continues forth. She leads the way in prayer and humility while reminding others that through Christ, justice is possible.

CONTEMPORARY PRAXIS

Submission is a critical spiritual practice on the road to justice. Without surrender to Jesus, Christians will not be able to tap into the power of God, which transforms all things: "And we all, who with unveiled faces contemplate the Lord's glory, are being transformed into his image with ever-increasing glory, which comes from the Lord, who is the Spirit" (2 Cor 3:18). Jesus, through his death on the cross, models perfect submission: the willingness to give his life for the sake of the world.

We see submission exemplified in the life of Oscar Romero, who was caught in the harsh struggle between the ruling elite of El Salvador and the priestly call on his life to serve the people. Particularly after the death of Father Grande, Romero used his power to call for justice and to speak boldly to the abusive authorities of his day. Archbishop Romero willingly paid the ultimate sacrifice for the people of El Salvador, giving his life as an act of submission to the God he served.

As we consider how submission equates with justice-oriented movements, it is important to acknowledge the ways Christians have sometimes abused this discipline. Richard Foster writes about this reality and reminds followers of Christ: "[Submission] is a posture obligatory upon *all* Christians: men as well as women, fathers as well as children, masters as well as slaves. We are commanded to live a life of submission because Jesus lived a life of submission, not because we are in a particular place or station in life. Self-denial is a posture fitting for all those who follow the crucified Lord."[59] All of us are called to mutual submission as a means of loving God and loving one another. We are called to "submit to one another out of reverence for Christ" (Eph 5:21).

As followers of Christ, we are called to be servants of one another and the world. Self-denial, through the spiritual practice of submission, is one of the differentiating features of Christian obedience and discipline. Christians follow the example of Jesus by coming alongside of people who suffer from poverty, oppression and injustice. Christian leaders such as Oscar Romero and Alexia

Salvatierra, who are willing to commit their lives to the spiritual practice of submission, provide inspiring examples.

◆ Giving Over to God as Submission

I first read about this exercise in a book by Mary Richardson called *Everything Is an Obsession to Me*. She described struggling with codependency and the need for control in her personal life and her relationships with others. This exercise is one of the ways she practices submission to God.

To begin, take several small sheets of paper. On each individual sheet of paper, write some burden or responsibility that is heavy on your heart. Some examples might include the monthly bills, conflict with a colleague, your relationship with your spouse or a particular meeting or activity. Start this exercise with a prayer asking God to help discern how to better enter into submission. After you have written something on all of the strips of paper, consider and pray over each one. Then take two cups: one cup represents issues you can do something about and situations that you need to take action on, and the other cup represents things you need to give over to God and situations over which you have no control. As you discern which strips of paper should go in which cup, you are practicing submitting things to God.

At first this exercise may seem silly or simplistic, but in reality it can be quite profound. Sometimes we want to control the universe around us. By putting things outside of our control in the cup that belongs to God, we receive a tangible reminder that he is the Lord of the universe. Of course, things that are in "our" cup can be submitted to God, too. The difference is that there is something that we can do about those situations. Let's say that you have gotten into an argument with a colleague at work and haven't yet apologized for the way you lost your patience. That situation should be put into your cup, and you might look for an opportunity that day to ask for forgiveness. But if you have already apologized and your colleague is holding a grudge, you should put that in God's cup, submitting the situation to him and asking for his intervention.

This exercise of submission has practical implications when reflecting about issues of injustice. Activists and advocates often feel responsible to work toward positive change. Practice this exercise while considering societal problems or injustices and whether or not there are actions you can take to make a difference.

◆ *Self-Denial as Submission*

The story of Oscar Romero highlights self-denial as a component of spiritual submission. Self-denial is the freedom to give ourselves away to others. It is a way we "take up our cross" to follow in the footsteps of Jesus. Self-denial can be exercised in very particular practices of spiritual formation, including fasting. Fasting is a physical denial of self that usually involves abstaining from food. Throughout the Scriptures, Jesus practiced fasting. If you have never fasted before, I would recommend starting with a day (or two or three days at most). In addition, it is important to drink water or other liquids. I would also recommend talking to your family doctor before practicing this particular discipline. Fasting can be a healthy exercise, but it is good to have a professional offer advice about the best way to proceed. Fasting is a physical exercise of self-denial that strips the body of comfort for a short period of time. As one cleanses the body, one's mind, heart and soul are submitted to God. Fasting can be a profound spiritual experience and an opportunity for further intimacy with God, because it reminds us that we are wholly dependent upon him.

◆ *Service as Submission*

Richard Foster writes, "In submission we are at last free to value other people. Their dreams and plans become important to us. We have entered into a new, wonderful, glorious freedom—the freedom to give up our own rights for the good of others."[60] Service is another exercise of submission to one another in Christ. As Jesus washed the feet of his disciples, he was serving them. We are called to follow in the footsteps of Jesus: to love and serve one another as an act of submission. God calls us to voluntary submission and to servanthood with one another. Consider an active way you can serve people in your immediate community and beyond.

◆ Confession as Submission

Many Catholics regularly practice the discipline of confession, and Protestants could learn a lot from this tradition. Dietrich Bonhoeffer says of confession: "Confession is thus a genuine part of the life of the saints, and one of the gifts of grace."[61] Confession is a conscious act of repenting of sin by sharing one's shortcomings and failures with someone else. First, one must prepare one's soul by submitting it to the care of the Holy Spirit. This process of self-examination allows time to truly reflect about the nature, thoughts, words and action of sin that have created separateness from God. A person must overcome self-denial and gain a new understanding of one's brokenness. Repentance is required for individual sin but also for acknowledgment of brokenness in the world and participation in unjust systems. Another part of the process is empathizing with how the sin has damaged or harmed others. State the intention to act differently and change the behavior in the future. Finally, a significant part of confession is embracing the gift of God's grace, knowing that we are completely forgiven because of the person of Christ.[62]

8

Courage, Joy and Celebration

Joy is at the heart of God himself.
We will never understand the significance of joy in human
life until we understand its importance to God. I suspect that
most of us seriously underestimate God's capacity for joy.

JOHN ORTBERG[1]

JUSTICE-ORIENTED MOVEMENTS must be inspired by God and deeply rooted in Christian spiritual practices and discipline. Otherwise, the popularity of justice-focused ideas will only be a "flash in the pan" and not long-lasting pursuit of societal change. The longevity and future of the church's success at bringing about effective change within society must be undergirded by the contemplative practices of silence, prayer, study of Scripture, community, worship, observance of the sabbath and submission. These disciplines provide the framework by which true and lasting change can occur. This concluding chapter reflects on how these disciplines are integrated and invites us into a life full of courage, joy and celebration.

COURAGE

Courage is one of the common attributes of the heroes of faith
mentioned in this book. For example, Mother Teresa had courage
to face her own personal dark night of the soul. King had courage
to stand firm against segregation and white supremacy rampant
throughout the South and other parts of the United States. And
Bishop Tutu speaks of courage in facing the oppression of apartheid:
"All of us experience fear, but when we confront and acknowledge
it, we are able to turn it into courage. Being courageous does not
mean never being scared; it means acting as you know you must
even though you are undeniably afraid."[2]

My father, Michael, is one of the most courageous people I
know. As a young man, he had a rough time making sense of life.
He made poor choices, stole things and was continually getting
into trouble. Embittered at the world, at age eighteen he volun-
teered to go to Vietnam to serve his country. After two tours, he
returned to the United States and fell in love with my mother. Determined to finish college, he attended classes at Towson State in
Baltimore. In a philosophy class, he was introduced to the person
of Jesus and had a profound conversion experience. He frequently
tells the story about how his introduction to Christ put his entire
life on a different course. He began to live differently. He often
went back to people he had stolen from and paid them what he
owed. He was determined to be faithful to this new call on his life
by expressing the love of God toward people.

Eventually, Dad had the opportunity to go to work for my grandfather who owned a lumber construction company. Over the course
of several years, he worked his way up from menial labor to the
manager of the truss plant. Eventually he became the president of
the company and bought my grandfather's business. In addition to
his hard work, he was determined to care for the people who

worked for him. Continually he put their needs ahead of his own. Over the course of several years of running the family business, my dad provided work for people who seemed to have no other opportunities. He gave work to people struggling with alcoholism, depression and other challenges. In years of recession, he went without a salary while being sure to pay the rest of the employees first. As I have watched my dad's leadership, I have been continually humbled by his commitment to do the right thing—regardless of the cost—and put others ahead of himself.

As I think about what it means to have courage in the face of life's challenges, my dad's selfless leadership continues to be an example. In August 2012, my father was diagnosed with stage III lung cancer. He has been very healthy, and an active runner, for most of his life. He has never smoked. When he received the diagnosis, the doctors connected the illness to his tour in Vietnam. He had been exposed excessively to the carcinogenic herbicide Agent Orange, which doctors say caused his deterioration in health. As my dad began the course of treatment for cancer—daily radiation for a period of seven or eight weeks and two different types of chemotherapy once a month—he did not express fear. Instead he got his life in order and began to establish a plan in case he does not live through the treatment. As we talked about his health, and perhaps his approaching death, he told me that when the time comes he will be ready to go and be with Jesus. He loves his family but is not afraid. Rather, he desires to be faithful with the many blessings God has given him, and to approach the next stage of life with great courage and peace.

JOY

Courage is often present in confrontations against injustice. Similarly, joy manifests itself when the power and presence of God penetrate this world. Some people naturally exude the presence of God through a joyful spirit. For others, becoming joyful may require a more intentional process. John Ortberg affirms, "We have greatly underestimated the necessity of joy." Being reminded of the words of Scripture—"the joy of the Lord is your strength" (Neh 8:10)—we must then assume that the absence of joy "will create weakness."[3] Joy, then, is a source of power and another means of connecting us with the heart of God. Not only do justice-oriented activists exemplify courage; they also connect deeply with God through the expression of joy.

Princess Kasune Zulu, a Christian activist, speaker and advocate from Zambia, is one of the most joyful people I know. Her countenance exudes joy. Her vibrancy and enthusiasm for life regularly reminds me that joy is one of the fruits of the spirit (Gal 5:22). Yet when one learns about Princess Zulu's story, her reason for joy might not be readily apparent.

When Princess was ten years old, she was forced from her comfortable city home into a mud hut in a remote dusty village for the next nine years. By the time she was eighteen, she had nursed her parents to their early and painful deaths and had been forced to marry a man twenty-five years her senior. At twenty-one years old, having birthed two daughters, she discovered she had HIV, a potentially lethal and incurable disease.[4] Today, Princess Zulu has committed her life to fighting on behalf of others. She is a world-known speaker and activist with strength, courage and great joy. She met with former President George W. Bush to ask him to dedicate $15 billion to fighting the AIDS epidemic across Africa. This is just one of the opportunities she has had in speaking truth to power. Princess Zulu's remarkable story is recounted in *Warrior Princess: Fighting for Life with Courage and Hope*.[5] She speaks not only of her own struggle but the effects of HIV and AIDS on hundreds of thousands of lives throughout the world. Princess is an example of someone who practices just spirituality through the disciplines of both courage and joy.

CELEBRATION

Celebration is another essential spiritual discipline. Celebration acknowledges God's provision at different points on our journey. It is the intentional act of taking pause on behalf of things that bring us joy. John Ortberg defines celebration as an activity that "brings pleasure—gathering with people we love, eating and drinking, singing and dancing. Spiritual celebration means doing them while reflecting on the wonderful God who has given us such wonderful gifts."[6] As one considers injustices in the world including suffering, poverty and oppression, celebration becomes particularly important.

The discipline of celebration may be particularly difficult for those whose work involves responding to suffering and pain in the world. What does it mean to have the "joy of the Lord" when spending time with poor street children in rural Upper Egypt? What does it mean to celebrate when working with people who are homeless in Chicago? Ortberg reminds us: "Often it is the people closest to suffering who have the most powerful joy."[7] This sense of joy and celebration can be seen readily in the African American worship tradition. I was once attending a friend's church on the south side of Chicago. His mother, a *madea*, was approaching her ninetieth birthday.[i] When the worship music began, she rose up out of her seat and began to dance. She couldn't move very quickly, but her feet shuffled back and forth in a radiant dance of joy and celebration. I couldn't help but think that her celebratory worship was a perfect example of experiencing joy in the Lord.

One way to practice the discipline of celebration is to set aside time each week to reflect upon happenings in life for which you are thankful. Dietrich Bonhoeffer practiced this discipline even when he was in prison. He experienced the communal meals with others

---

[i]*Madea* is a term of endearment used commonly in the African American tradition. It refers to one's biological mother or a woman who plays a similar role.

as an opportunity for joy: "Through our daily meals He is calling us to rejoice, to keep holiday in the midst of our working day."[8] Celebration can include listening to music you love, reading books that refresh your spirit or surrounding yourself with things of beauty. Ortberg encourages: "Take the time to experience and savor joy, then direct your heart toward God so that you can come to *know* he is the giver of 'every good and perfect gift.'"[9]

Another way to practice the spiritual discipline of celebration is by lighting a victory candle. My spiritual mentor Sibyl Towner introduced me to this practice. For a special occasion, Sibyl gave my husband and me a small notebook with the following passage written on its cover: "May we shout for joy over your victory and lift up our banners in the name of our God. May the Lord grant all your requests" (Ps 20:5). Her idea was that we could use the notebook to record any special celebrations in our lives. When something special happened for my husband, me or our loved ones, we would write it down with a date in the victory notebook. We would then light the candle and say a prayer of thanksgiving. Over the years, the victory notebook has become a special place of remembering the work of God in our lives. A few times a year, we pull out the notebook and read through it to remember and celebrate the good things that God has done. There is good reason for us to celebrate. God is at work in the world.

Efrem Smith: The Integration of Just Spirituality

Efrem Smith is a mentor, friend and example to me in my own life and ministry. He models "just spirituality": a holistic manifestation of the gospel that speaks of God's heart for the world through evangelism, justice and integrated spiritual practice. Smith was raised in the black church. He says, "It's hard to grow up in the black church and an urban context and to not have a justice orientation and theology."[10] He identifies the urban Park Avenue United Methodist Church in Minneapolis as playing a significant role in shaping his personal engagement in justice. In college, he spent every summer working at Park Avenue, where he learned about community development and justice ministries while working with at-risk youth. Eventually, he became the executive director of the Park Avenue Foundation, the community development arm of the church, which hosts a health clinic, legal clinic, computer learning center and job programs. Smith learned at Park Avenue the importance of the church's engagement in both spiritual formation and social action within society. Since then, Smith has served as the founding pastor of Sanctuary Covenant Church and president of the Sanctuary Community Development Corporation in Minneapolis. He now serves as superintendent of the Pacific Southwest Conference of the Evangelical Covenant Church.

Sanctuary Covenant was founded in 2003 as an evangelical, multiracial, urban church with a community development component. It models the holistic call of the gospel to live out Matthew 28 (making disciples of all nations) through the church and Matthew 25 (responding to the needs of the least of these) through community development. Sanctuary Community Development Corporation was created to address racial and class disparities through economic and youth development. Today, as the superintendent of the Pacific Southwest Conference, Smith leads more than one hundred churches and encourages them in initiatives of compassion, mercy and justice. He believes denominations will only be relevant if they are willing and able to resource pastors and equip them for church growth, evangelism, compassion and justice.

Efrem Smith's own life was deeply influenced by many other leaders, including John Perkins, Tony Campolo and Tom Skinner. "Their sermons and their writing had a tremendous impact on my own personal development," he says. Later, he was significantly influenced by the writings of Howard Thurman and Martin Luther King Jr.

Smith's example is an important one because he has not only practiced and led significant movements of community change and development, but because he has also pastored a successful and growing church through intentional discipleship and evangelism. When I talked to Smith about his own connection with God, he mentioned several components including spiritual disciplines, mentoring and spiritual direction. Spiritual direction and submission to a group of diverse advisors is one of the main personal practices for Smith. He says, "All too often spiritual directors simply reinforce our false understanding of where we think God is leading us." Thus, Smith encourages a diverse group of advisors. He also identifies racial reconciliation as a spiritual discipline. He says: "Justice ministry ought to be an overflowing of a deepening, reconciling relationship with God."

Regular daily reflection in the Word of God is important for Smith. He encourages people not to be legalistic about the practice. For some people, a concentrated fifteen or twenty minutes on the same text in a row can be a powerful meditative experience. However, Smith says, at times he needs to "sit in a chapter or a book for a long period of time," a practice that allows the truth of God's Word to "take deep root in the soil of my soul." In addition to reading the Scriptures, Smith takes one full day a month for intentional time alone with God. In addition, he regularly takes an extended retreat of two or three days during which he can be alone, in silence, and meditate in the Scriptures. He describes the importance in his own personal journey of having direct and regular experiences in "locations that cry out for justice." Thus, he will often take his retreats in Los Angeles, Oakland or another community that helps him connect directly with economic disparities and the need for justice. He says of these experiences, "Scripture deepens in my bones when the location is relevant to the text." This was powerful for Martin Luther King Jr., for Mother Teresa and for other leaders of faith in this book. Smith continues, "The Scriptures had life because these people read them in a jail cell, or with the threat of death, or in the midst of disease, suffering and a poverty-stricken environment." Smith challenges: "If we only read the Scriptures in the context of a nice suburban Starbucks, the Scriptures keep safe . . . and we might be missing something."

One of the things I talked to Smith about is whether there is a difference between Christian movements of justice and secular ones. He said, "At the end of the day, secular justice lacks power . . . the power that comes from the Holy Spirit and comes from God." Explaining his understanding of justice-oriented movements, Smith said, "Fighting for justice is not just a physical battle; it is a spiritual battle against principalities, powers and spirits." Thus, spiritual weapons are needed for success. Spiritual disciplines allow people to be equipped to fight spiritual battles. Ephesians 6:10-11 reminds us to "be strong in the Lord and in his mighty power" and to "put on the full armor of God." Smith and other leaders like him remind us that Christians must be equipped to tackle both the material and spiritual aspects of quests for justice.

BENEDICTION TO JUST SPIRITUALITY

Spiritual disciplines are critical as we seek to be agents of God's justice in the world. Silence and prayer become sources of power that connect us directly to God and the movement of his Spirit. Scripture becomes a weapon that informs our strategy of advocating for justice. The community around us hones our skills and holds us accountable when we are headed in the wrong direction. Worship reminds us that God is worthy to be adored and esteemed. Observation of the sabbath allows us to have sustainable rhythms of life that will keep us in the game over the long run. The discipline of submission draws us closer to the person of Christ as we follow his example and "take up our cross" in our pursuits of justice in the world. These spiritual practices shape and hone us into Christlikeness, confronting our pride and leading us toward humility. All the while God uses us, even in our brokenness, to make a difference in the world.

Mother Teresa reminds us: "Silence is at the root of our union with God and with one another."[11] Her intimate connection with God led her to live alongside of men, women and children who are poor. The love of God compelled her toward greater depths of compassion than most people can even seek to understand.

Dietrich Bonhoeffer practiced the spiritual discipline of prayer and remained faithful even when imprisoned for seeking to overturn the Nazi regime. Bishop Tutu concurs and emphasizes rhythm and space in the devotional life. He says: "The practice of prayer helps us to discern, from among the many voices we hear and choices we face each day, which is the guiding voice of God."[12] All of the justice leaders mentioned in *Just Spirituality* practice prayer as a means of connecting with God.

Watchman Nee committed his life to diligent study of the Word of God. As a result, his movement of evangelism spread throughout China leading up to the communist revolution. As he served years in prison, his commitment was an example to Christ-followers around the world of the importance of reading, studying and reflecting upon the Word of God.

Martin Luther King Jr.'s life and ministry was largely shaped and launched by the community of Montgomery. Community sharpens us and challenges us to be better individuals. King's advocacy for the rights of people of color is a reminder that we cannot move forward alone but must walk side by side with our brothers and sisters in Christ in order to bring about effective change. Desmond Tutu prompts us to remember the ways community helps us to connect with God: "Flaws and vulnerabilities can build the bridge to human community and to a relationship with the divine."[13] Because of community, we are not alone on the journey of being reconcilers and advocates of justice.

Fairuz's voice and music are a desperate cry for the freedom of Jerusalem and others around the world. Her personal piety and commitment to God inform her music and worship. Freedom movements around the globe use music as a tool for telling their story and crying to God for deliverance. Worship also reminds believers that God is powerful and in control; he is worthy of worship. Desmond Tutu speaks of God's love for the world as the underlying source of reconciliation. Sabbath, rest and healthy spiritual rhythms are necessary for tapping into the love of God. Sabbath is particularly important for men and women engaged in justice because it reminds us of the need for physical rest and soul nourishment.

Oscar Romero was a leading voice for the poor and oppressed in El Salvador. His life and ministry exemplified the spiritual discipline of submission even unto the ultimate sacrifice of giving his life. As a martyr, Romero's cry for justice on behalf of the poor in his country echoed around the world. His humble service modeled submission as he followed in the footsteps of Christ.

Each of these stories of heroes of the faith provides reminders of the critical need of Christians to daily practice the spiritual disciplines. The global contribution of these leaders is without question. For example, in 1998, Westminster Abbey decided to fill the ten niches on the West Façade with the statues of Christian martyrs from the twentieth century. Oscar Romero, Dietrich Bonhoeffer and Martin Luther King Jr. were included among those ten martyrs.[14] What do all of these leaders have in common? They were willing to sacrificially give of themselves on behalf of people who are suffering under the helm of injustice. Tutu describes the call of discipleship this way:

> Jesus reminds his disciples that they cannot stay basking in the glory of God on the mountaintop. They must go down into the

valley of human need. And so must we. But as we work to feed the hungry, we must also remember to draw our own sustenance from our glimpses of God. In all the activity that is required of us as God's partners, there must also be stillness, for in this stillness we can hear God's voice in our lives and the will of God working in the world.[15]

Spiritual disciplines are necessary to help us stay connected to God. As Christians seek to live out the gospel in the world, the disciplines keep us on track and allow the transforming power of God to work in our lives.

Each of these heroes of the faith gave of themselves on behalf of others. They were compelled by the love of God to make a difference in the world by responding to the injustices they encountered. Mother Teresa spoke of this type of giving: "Love is giving. God loved the world so much that He gave His Son. Jesus loved the world so much, loved you, loved me so much that He gave His life. And He wants us to love as He loved. And so now we have also to give until it hurts. True love is a giving and giving until it hurts."[16]

We, as Christ-followers, are given the opportunity to share the love of Jesus with the world. Wherever we are, whatever our circumstances, regardless of limited resources or wealth, God desires to use us as examples of his love and justice in the world. He desires intimate connection with us through silence, prayer and other spiritual practices. God wants to pour out his love to us and through us. As Christians, we can tap into the power of Christ's death and resurrection. God wants us to live out *just spirituality*. It is a great privilege that God empowers us to respond to oppression and injustice and to exercise his love and mercy in the world!

Acknowledgments

◆

THIS BOOK IS DEDICATED TO several men and women who seriously live out their convictions to be messengers of God's love and agents of God's justice. They are spiritual giants whose lives reflect intimacy with God and hope for his power and mercy at work in the world. I am significantly indebted to them for their care, attention and investment in my own life and ministry and in the lives of so many people upon whom they have had influence. Brother Romuald was my teacher at St. Mary's Ryken High School. He taught me more about a life of committed devotion than anything I could have learned in his challenging AP science and math classes! My great-aunt, Sister Francis Augusta, was a Benedictine nun who served as an educator from the time she joined the convent as a novice at thirteen years old. She was one of the most loving people I have ever known. Greg Jao and Tamarin Huelin walked me through the challenging years of college life at the University of Chicago. Greg's intelligence, rationality, and passion for the gospel provided a steady rock for me to lean on. Tamarin's love, sacrifice and patience offered me hope and encouragement when there didn't seem to be light at the end of the tunnel. At Willow Creek, I was introduced to many of the spiritual practices written about in this book. Sibyl Towner provided a gentle guide on how God's presence penetrates the most complex and challenging of life's circumstances. Gilbert Bilezikian has been an unbridled advocate offering support and affirmation of my gifts in leadership in immeasurable ways. Diane Grant has continually poured herself out on my behalf and expanded my understanding of the ways the Lord works through spiritual direction. Tom Getman has been an example to me because of his deep devotion to the Lord and his remarkable passion as an advocate of justice. It has been a great source of empowerment and comfort to have such incredible people walking with me as companions along this journey of life. I am deeply grateful for their mentoring and friendship.

I am also grateful to many who supported the writing of *Just Spirituality*. Al Hsu has consistently been a wonderful person to work with as my editor. Jenny Trees read through every chapter (several times!) and provided helpful feedback and encouragement. I sought the expertise, comments and wisdom of others on various chapters and topics: Soong-Chan Rah, William Yoo, Troy Jackson, Fady Eldiery, Andy Smith and Paul Haidostian. Any errors are my own.

As often is the case, the location where one writes provides the opportunity for time with God and an atmosphere of peace, quiet and reflection. I am thankful to the Pendle Hill Quaker retreat center in Pennsylvania; to Sister Lauren and the Benedictine Sisters in Elizabeth, NJ; and to my brother and sister-in-law Chas and Tricia Fisk in Washington.

I am also deeply indebted to my family. My husband, Roby, is the greatest supporter of my life, work and ministry. He continues to sacrifice so that I might be free to pursue my passions and calling. My parents never fail to consistently love me and believe in me. I certainly have not done anything to deserve the support and affection of so many amazing people. It is humbling to be the recipient of such powerful love.

Study Guide

Chapter 1
MOTHER TERESA: *From Silence to Service*

1. Have you had experience practicing silence? What was it like? Did God speak to you as you purposefully quieted your soul?

2. What do you think was the source of Mother Teresa's love and concern for the poor? How did her relationship with God influence her work and ministry? What do you think is the connection between silence and service?

3. What is the relationship between humility and silence? How can our stillness before God shape our understanding of self and the world? How does silence encourage us to respond to poverty and injustice?

4. What did you learn from the story of Sami Awad? Did you resonate with his experiences? How might his example of practicing silence apply to your life?

5. Take some time in silence—perhaps fifteen or twenty minutes—to reflect about God's purpose in your life. You may want to have crayons, pencils or other creative tools to draw a picture or to write out some of the things that come to your mind in the silence. Use the instructions in "Centering and Entering In" in chapter one to guide your experience. When you are finished, share your reflections.

6. How might God be calling you to incorporate silence into your spiritual practices and rhythm of life? If you haven't had the opportunity to practice the discipline of silence, make a commitment to spend some committed time being quiet before God during the next week. When you return to your group, share about the things you learned. What was challenging about the practice? Where, if at all, did you experience God speaking to you?

Chapter 2
DIETRICH BONHOEFFER: *From Prayer to Discipleship*

1. How do you think Bonhoeffer's background prepared him for his active role of resistance against Hitler's regime? How did the seminary at Finkenwalde influence his understanding of God and his exercise of spiritual practices?

2. What daily activities did Bonhoeffer practice as a part of his prayer and devotional life? What role did discipline play in his spiritual devotions?

3. What do you think Bonhoeffer meant by the "moral obligation to love"? How did this play out in his own life, particularly in his advocacy for the Jewish people under Nazi oppression?

4. How do Larry Martin and International Justice Mission incarnate the lessons Bonhoeffer taught and practiced?

5. What role does prayer play in supporting social action and activism against injustice? How might God be calling you and your community to more regularly practice prayer?

6. Close your time by praying together the Peacemakers' Litany at the end of chapter two.

Chapter 3
WATCHMAN NEE: *From Study to Evangelism*

1. What do you think about the correlation between signs and wonders and effective evangelism? You might want to reflect about the story of John Wimber and the Vineyard or to talk about your own experiences with manifestations of the Holy Spirit. Does anyone in the group have a story they want to share?

2. Were you familiar with Watchman Nee and his ministry? What did you learn about his life and influence? What were some of the effects of the Little Flock movement?

3. What did Nee teach about the significance of God's Word? How did his view of Christ's death and resurrection influence his life and ministry?

4. What did Nee teach his disciples about the need for evangelism? What things did they do to share the love of Christ and the message of the gospel with people throughout China?

5. What did you learn from Mark Labberton's story and example? How does Labberton connect what Scripture teaches about evangelism with God's commandments to pursue justice?

6. Choose one of the exercises in chapter three to practice together as a group—the inductive Bible study, creative discovery of God's Word, *lectio divina* or memory verses. Choose a passage such as James 2:14-24 about God's call to social action and justice. Commit to completing the exercise over a period of time. What did you learn? How did God's Word come alive and speak to you in your study?

7. What do you think the relationship is between God's commandment to love your neighbor and God's heart for justice? How might God be calling you to study his Word, evangelize and respond to the needs in your community?

Chapter 4
MARTIN LUTHER KING JR.: *From Community to Proclamation*

1. When have you experienced a profound sense of Christian community? What was it like? If you haven't experienced it, what do you think biblical community or sacred companions should look like?

2. What does Gilbert Bilezikian write and teach about biblical community? Do you agree? How do you think the church practices God-centered community? How can the church carry out its mission to be a biblical community? What types of things can we do to positively contribute?

3. What is King's idea of beloved community? What does it look like, and what purpose does it play?

4. How did King experience community in Montgomery? How did his relationships and experiences in Montgomery affect his ministry as a preacher and advocate of equality and justice?

5. What type of vision did King proclaim? What was the source of his vision? Where do you resonate with his proclamation? Where might you disagree?

6. How did King's sermons influence a movement of social change? How does this relate to your community and circumstances today?

7. What stuck out to you in Gary Burge's story and experiences? Did you resonate? How does community influence Burge in his academic work and ministry?

8. What kind of relationship do you have in community and the local church? How do you think God might desire to strengthen those relationships? What types of things might God be calling you to do in this regard?

9. All of us have had experiences of brokenness within the context of community. If you feel comfortable doing so, share your past experience with others and ask God to heal the brokenness that resulted from your painful encounter. If someone in the group shares a painful experience, enter into prayer together, asking for God's healing and intervention.

Chapter 5
FAIRUZ: *From Worship to Freedom*

1. Have you had a worship experience during which you felt the presence of God powerfully? What was it like? How did you experience God?

2. Do you resonate with the stories of how worship became a declaration of justice during the civil rights movement and other quests for freedom? Why or why not?

3. What did you learn from the story of Fairuz and her influence in Lebanon, the Arab world and beyond? How does Fairuz associate Christ's death and resurrection with the Arab quest for freedom?

4. How do you define worship? What elements, other than music, are components of creatively engaging in worship of the Creator?

5. How did Wenche Miriam use her gifts of music to worship God while serving others? Were you inspired by her story? Why or why not?

6. As a group, commit to practice a creative exercise of worship. Perhaps it is a spiritually guided tour, sharing an art journal or hosting a worship night focused on caring for people in need in your community. After the experience, reflect about the things you learned and how you experienced God.

Chapter 6
DESMOND TUTU: *From Sabbath to Reconciliation*

1. What do you think the Genesis narrative teaches us about the significance of rest and sabbath?

2. What role did Desmond Tutu play in dismantling apartheid in South Africa? How did his spiritual connection to God influence his views of reconciliation and justice?

3. According to Tutu, how does observation of the sabbath connect us to the love of God?

4. What are the biblical notions of shalom, sabbath and the year of Jubilee? What do they teach us about the nature of God, the rhythms he wants us to experience and our relationship to the rest of his creation?

5. What does the story of Daniel Hill teach us about our role as agents of justice in our communities? Does God need us to accomplish his will and purpose in the world? What does observation of the sabbath teach us about ourselves and God?

6. If you are able, commit to practicing sabbath one day a week for at least a month. After your fourth observation of sabbath, reflect on whether you have noticed a difference in your perspective on self, God and the world. What have you learned? Was it difficult to practice the spiritual discipline of rest? How did your observations influence your perspective of injustice and needs in your community? If you are not doing so already, commit to incorporating sabbath into your life rhythms on a more regular basis.

Chapter 7
OSCAR ROMERO: *From Submission to Martyrdom*

1. As you reflect on the story at the Louisiana State Penitentiary at Angola, consider whether you have ever observed or experienced Christian submission. What was it like? What was unique about the experience?

2. What did you learn from Oscar Romero's story? How did his life change after the death of his friend Father Rio Grande? What was the shift in his relationship with the powers and authorities in El Salvador and the Catholic Church?

3. What was the source of power and conviction in Romero's life? How did his relationship with God influence the choices that he made and his leadership?

4. What does Romero's ministry teach us about God's heart for the poor and God's heart for justice?

5. How was the discipline of submission practiced in Romero's life? What can we learn from his example?

6. What did you learn from Alexia Salvatierra's story? What is the source of her courage and conviction? Where does the energy for her activism come from?

7. Are there places in your own life where God might be calling you to enter into the discipline of submission? How and in what ways? How might your community of friends and believers support you in this endeavor?

Chapter 8
COURAGE, JOY AND CELEBRATION

1. Why is it important for justice-oriented movements to be rooted in spiritual disciplines?

2. How did the Christian leaders mentioned throughout the book exemplify courage? Do you think courage is an important element in responding to global injustice? Why or why not?

3. Did you relate to the story about Michael Cannon? How did his actions exemplify courage? Who is someone you know who is courageous? How might God be calling you to be courageous in your own life?

4. Why is the spiritual discipline of joy important? Do you know someone like Princess Zulu, who has the spiritual gift of joy? What is it like to be around that person? How might you better express joy in the Lord in your own life?

5. How would you define celebration, and why is it an important component of our spiritual journey? Are there ways you and your family or friends currently practice the discipline of celebration? Are there other things you could do to celebrate the work of God in your lives?

6. What components of the spiritual journey do you see exemplified in Efrem Smith and his life and ministry? How does his story show how the different spiritual disciplines can be integrated in the context of social action?

7. How has the study of justice-oriented disciplines caused you to reflect on your own relationship with God? Are there specific disciplines or practices you would like to better integrate into your own life? If so, how? Share your commitments with a friend or small group for the purpose of mutual encouragement.

Notes

INTRODUCTION: *Spiritual Practices as Fuel for the Soul*

[1]Dănuţ Mănăstireanu, ed., *People of Faith, People of Justice* (Iaşi, Romania: Adoramus Publishers, 2010), p. 6.

[2]Richard J. Foster, *Streams of Living Water: Celebrating the Great Traditions of Christian Faith* (San Francisco: HarperCollins, 1998), p. 176.

[3]Ibid., p. 179.

[4]Mother Teresa, *Love: The Words and Inspiration of Mother Teresa* (Boulder, Colo.: Blue Mountain Press, 2007), cover.

[5]Dietrich Bonhoeffer, *Christ the Center*, trans. Edwin H. Robertson (New York: HarperCollins, 1978), p. 27.

[6]Mother Teresa, *No Greater Love* (New York: New World Library, 2002), p. 10.

Chapter 1
MOTHER TERESA: *From Silence to Service*

[1]Mother Teresa, *Love: The Words and Inspiration of Mother Teresa* (Boulder, Colo.: Blue Mountain Press, 2007), p. 3.

[2] Ibid., p. 331.

[3]Mother Teresa, *No Greater Love* (New York: New World Library, 2002), p. 10.

[4]Brian Kolodiejchuk, *Mother Teresa: Come Be My Light, The Private Writings of the Saint of Calcutta* (New York: Doubleday, 2007), p. 15.

[5]"Mother Teresa of Calcutta (1910-1997)," Vatican website, accessed August 3, 2012 <www.vatican.va/news_services/liturgy/saints/ns_lit_doc_20031019_ madre-teresa_en.html>.

[6]Mary S. Poplin, *Finding Calcutta: What Mother Teresa Taught Me About Meaningful Work and Service* (Downers Grove, Ill.: InterVarsity Press, 2008), p. 294.

[7]Mother Teresa, *Love*, p. 22.

[8]Ibid., p. 3.

[9]Ibid., p. 30.

[10]Mother Teresa, *No Greater Love*, p. 8.

[11]Mother Teresa, *Love*, p. 15.

[12]Poplin, *Finding Calcutta*, p. 299.

[13]Kolodiejchuk, *Mother Teresa*, p. 197.

[14]Ibid., p. 188.

[15]Ibid., p. 396n26.

[16]Ibid., p. 197.

[17]Mother Teresa, *The Book of Peace: Finding the Spirit in a Busy World*, excerpted from *A Simple Path*, compiled by Lucinda Vardey (London: Random House, 1996), p. 5.

[18]Mother Teresa, *No Greater Love*, p. 9.

[19]Mother Teresa, *Love*, pp. 16-18.

[20]Mother Teresa, *No Greater Love*, p. 8.

[21]Mother Teresa, *Love*, pp. 60-61.

[22]Ibid., pp. 19-20, 81.

[23]Ibid., p. 142.

[24]Ibid., p. 77.

[25]Mother Teresa, *No Greater Love*, pp. 8, 54.

[26]Mother Teresa, *Love*, p. 329.

[27]Mother Teresa, *Book of Peace*, p. 85.

[28]Poplin, *Finding Calcutta*, p. 287.

[29]Ibid., pp. 14, 293.

[30]Mother Teresa, *Love*, p. 108.

[31]Ibid., p. 88.

[32]Mother Teresa, *No Greater Love*, p. 175.

[33]Mother Teresa, *Book of Peace*, p. 57.

[34]Sami Awad, interview with author, September 13, 2011. Unless otherwise noted, all quotations from Sami Awad in this section are from the same interview.

[35]Sami Awad, "Giving 1 Percent of Jesus to Somalia," *The Huffington Post*, September 12, 2011 <http://www.huffingtonpost.com/sami-awad/christian-social-justice-somalia_b_947160.html>.

[36]Foster, *Streams of Living Water*, p. 98.

[37]Ibid., pp. 22, 143.

[38]Adele Ahlberg Calhoun, *Spiritual Disciplines Handbook: Practices that Transform Us* (Downers Grover, Ill.: InterVarsity Press, 2005), p. 109.

[39]Calhoun, *Spiritual Disciplines*, p. 108.

[40]Mother Teresa, *Love*, p. 3.

[41]Richard Foster, *Celebration of Discipline: The Path to Spiritual Growth* (New York: HarperSanFrancisco, 1988), and Ruth Haley Barton, *Invitation to Solitude and Silence: Experiencing God's Transforming Presence* (Downers Grove, Ill.: InterVarsity Press, 2004).

[42]Foster, *Celebration of Discipline*, p. 108.

[43]Poplin, p. 299.

[44]Teresa, *No Greater Love*, p. 54.

[45]Foster, *Celebration of Discipline*, p. 30.

[46]Calhoun, *Spiritual Disciplines*, pp. 108-109.

[47]John Ortberg, *The Life You've Always Wanted* (Grand Rapids: Zondervan, 1997), p. 81.

[48]Ibid., p. 87.

Chapter 2
DIETRICH BONHOEFFER: *From Prayer to Discipleship*

[1]Eric Metaxas, *Bonhoeffer: Pastor, Martyr, Prophet, Spy* (Nashville, Tenn.: Thomas Nelson, 2010), p. 449.

[2]Dietrich Bonhoeffer, *Life Together: A Discussion of Christian Fellowship*, trans. John W. Doberstein (New York: Harper & Row Publishers, 1954), p. 9.

[3]Dǎnuţ Mǎnǎstireanu, ed., *People of Faith, People of Justice* (Iaşi, Romania: Adoramus Publishers, 2010), p. 54.

[4]Dietrich Bonhoeffer, *Meditating on the Word*, trans. David McI. Gracie (New York: Cowley Publications, 1986), p. 25.

[5]Ibid.

[6]Dietrich Bonhoeffer, *Christ the Center*, trans. Edwin H. Robertson (New York: HarperCollins, 1978), p. 20.

[7]Mǎnǎstireanu, *People of Faith*, p. 54.

[8]Bonhoeffer, *Meditating on the Word*, p. 25.

[9]Dietrich Bonhoeffer, *Life Together: A Discussion of Christian Fellowship*, trans. Dohn W. Doberstein (New York: Harper & Row Publishers, 1954), p. 10.

[10]Bonhoeffer, *Christ at the Center*, p. 18.

[11]Bonhoeffer, *Meditating on the Word*, p. 31.

[12]Bonhoeffer, *Life Together*, p. 12.

[13]Mǎnǎstireanu, *People of Faith*, p. 54.

[14]Ibid.

[15]Dietrich Bonhoeffer, *Letters and Papers from Prison*, ed. Eberhard Bethge (New York: Simon & Schuster, 1953), pp. 135, 139.

[16]Ibid., p. 139.

[17]Bonhoeffer, *Life Together*, p. 75.

[18]Bonhoeffer, *Letters and Papers from Prison*, p. 149.

[19]Mǎnǎstireanu, *People of Faith*, p. 54.

[20]Dietrich Bonhoeffer, *Ethics*, ed. Eberhard Bethge (New York: Simon & Schuster, 1955), p. 46.

[21]Bonhoeffer, *Meditating on the Word*, p. 16.

[22]Dietrich Bonhoeffer, *The Cost of Discipleship* (New York: Simon & Schuster, 1995), p. 149.

[23]Bonhoeffer, *Meditating on the Word*, p. 92.

[24]Ibid., pp. 128-29.

[25]Richard J. Foster, *Streams of Living Water: Celebrating the Great Traditions of Christian Faith* (San Francisco: HarperCollins, 1998), p. 77.

[26]Bonhoeffer, *Meditating on the Word*, p. 7.

[27]Metaxas, *Bonhoeffer*, p. 12.

[28]Bonhoeffer, *Meditating on the Word*, p. 9.

[29]Bonhoeffer, *Cost of Discipleship*, p. 163, 166.

[30]Ibid., pp. 163, 165.

[31]Ibid., p. 163.

[32]Foster, *Streams of Living Water*, p. 173.

[33]Bonhoeffer, *Meditating on the Word*, p. 35.

[34]Bonhoeffer, *Life Together*, p. 64.

[35]Bonhoeffer, *Cost of Discipleship*, p. 162.

[36]Bonhoeffer, *Life Together*, p. 64.

[37]Bonhoeffer, *Cost of Discipleship*, p. 170.

[38]Bonhoeffer, *Life Together*, p. 73.

[39]Ibid., pp. 61, 64.

[40]Bonhoeffer, *Cost of Discipleship*, p. 165.

[41]Ibid., p. 167.

[42]"Who We Are," International Justice Mission, accessed December 10, 2011, <http://www.ijm.org/who-we-are>.

[43]Larry Martin, email message to author, July 27, 2011.

[44]Larry Martin, interview with author, August 9, 2011.

[45]Ibid.

[46]Gary Haugen, Leadership Institute for Transformation Project (LIFT) video clip, Willow Creek Association (2011).

[47]Larry Martin, email message.

[48]Larry Martin, interview.

[49]Ibid.

[50]Ibid.

[51]Haugen, LIFT Project video clip.

[52]Larry Martin, email message.

[53]Ibid.

[54]Ibid.

[55]Bonhoeffer, *Meditating on the Word*, p. 33.

[56]Bonhoeffer, *Cost of Discipleship*, p. 163.

[57]Ibid., p. 187.

[58]Quotations in this paragraph from Bonhoeffer, *Meditating on the Word*, p. 34.

[59]Adapted from a prayer by Pastor Jack Knox, Salem (Ore.) Mennonite Church. Used with permission.

[60]Bonhoeffer, *Meditating on the Word*, p. 13.

[61]Ibid., pp. 5-6.

[62]Metaxas, *Bonhoeffer*, p. 369.

[63]Bonhoeffer, *Christ the Center*, p. 27.

[64]Bonhoeffer, *Cost of Discipleship*, p. 164.

[65]Quotations in this section from Father Thomas Ryan, sermon, World Vision U.S. staff chapel, Washington, D.C., November 30, 2011.

Chapter 3
WATCHMAN NEE: *From Study to Evangelism*

[1]Watchman Nee, *Changed into His Likeness* (Racine, Wis.: Treasures Media Inc., 2006), Kindle edition, Kindle locations 943-47.

[2]John Wimber with Kevin Springer, *Power Evangelism* (London: Hodder and Stoughton, 1992), p. 10.

[3]Wimber, *Power Evangelism*, p. 78.

[4]Nee, *Changed into His Likeness*, Kindle locations 381-87.

[5]Bob Laurent, *Watchman Nee: Man of Suffering* (Uhrichsville, Ohio: Barbour Publishing, Inc., 1998), p. 18.

[6]Ibid., p. 23.

[7]Ibid., p. 39.

[8]Ibid., p. 85.

[9]Ibid., p. 157.

[10]Ibid., p. 35.

[11]Ibid., pp. 47-48.

[12]Ibid., p. 114.

[13]Ibid., p. 105.

[14]Ibid., pp. 123-124.

[15]Ibid., p. 146.

[16]Ibid., p. 64.

[17]Ibid., p. 65.

[18]Ibid., p. 147.

[19]Ibid., p. 162.

[20]Ibid., p. 162.

[21]Ibid., p. 154.

[22]Ibid., p. 154.

[23]Ibid., p. 168.

[24]Ibid., p. 170.

[25]Ibid., p. 173.

[26]Ibid., p. 7.

[27]Ibid., p. 174.

[28]Ibid., p. 86.

[29]Watchman Nee, *The Latent Power of the Soul* (New York: Christian Fellowship Publishers, Inc., 1972), p. 8.

[30]Ibid., pp. 15, 19.

[31]Laurent, *Watchman Nee*, p. 39.

[32]Watchman Nee, *Spiritual Discernment* (New York: Christian Fellowship Publishers, Inc., 2010), Kindle edition, Kindle locations 612-22.

[33]Ibid., Kindle locations 612-22.

[34]Ibid, Kindle locations 612-22.

[35]Ibid., Kindle locations 894-902.

[36]Ibid.

[37]Nee, *Latent Power*, p. 11.

[38]Ibid., p. 19.

[39]Ibid., p. 36.

[40]Ibid., pp. 21, 30, 35.

[41]Ibid., p. 26.

[42]Laurent, *Watchman Nee*, p. 141.

[43]Nee, *Changed into His Likeness*, Kindle locations 214-19.

[44]Laurent, *Watchman Nee*, p. 108.

[45]Ibid., p. 99.

[46]Ibid., p. 106.

[47]Ibid., p. 36.

[48]Ibid., p. 118.

[49]Ibid., p. 118.

[50]Ibid., p. 135.

[51]Mark Labberton, *The Dangerous Act of Worship: Living God's Call to Justice* (Downers Grove, Ill.: InterVarsity Press, 2007).

[52]Mark Labberton, interview with author, September 14, 2011. All quotations in this section are from this interview.

[53]Labberton, *Dangerous Act*, and *The Dangerous Act of Loving Your Neighbor: Seeing Others Through the Eyes of Jesus* (Downers Grove, Ill.: InterVarsity Press, 2010).

[54]For more on the Red Letter Christians, see <www.redletterchristians.org>.

[55]Gordon D. Fee and Douglas Stuart, *How to Read the Bible for All Its Worth: A Guide to Understanding the Bible* (Grand Rapids: Zondervan, 1993), p. 11.

[56]Lindsay Olesburg, *The Bible Study Handbook: A Comprehensive Guide to an Essential Practice* (Downers Grove, Ill.: InterVarsity Press, 2012).

[57]"Inductive Bible Study Hints," InterVarsity Christian Fellowship, accessed September 22, 2011, <http://www.intervarsity.org/bible-studies/inductive-bible-study-hints>. Suggestions in this section come from this website.

[58]James C. Wilhoit and Evan B. Howard, *Discovering Lectio Divina: Bringing Scripture into Ordinary Life* (Downers Grove, Ill.: InterVarsity Press, 2012).

Chapter 4

MARTIN LUTHER KING JR.: *From Community to Proclamation*

[1]James M. Washington, ed., *I Have a Dream: Writings and Speeches that Changed the World* (San Francisco: HarperCollins, 1992), pp. 27-28.

[2]David G. Benner, *Sacred Companions: The Gift of Spiritual Friendship and Direction* (Downers Grove, Ill.: InterVarsity Press, 2002), p. 15, emphasis in original.

[3]Gilbert Bilezikian, *Community 101: Reclaiming the Local Church as Community of Oneness* (Grand Rapids: Zondervan, 1997), p. 186.

[4]Ibid., p. 16.

[5]Benner, *Sacred Companions*, p. 14.

[6]Ibid., p. 17.

[7]This wisdom came from a conversation with Efrem Smith on September 13, 2011.

[8]Charles Marsh, *The Beloved Community: How Faith Shapes Social Justice, from the Civil Rights Movement to Today* (New York: Basic Books, 2005), p. 2.

[9]Ibid., p. 5.

[10]Ibid., p. 50.

[11]Ibid., p. 210.

[12]Ibid., p. 50.

[13]David J. Garrow, *Bearing the Cross: Martin Luther King, Jr., and the Southern Christian Leadership Conference* (New York: HarperCollins, 2004), p. 37.

[14]Ibid., p. 37.

[15]Troy Jackson, *Becoming King: Martin Luther King Jr. and the Making of a National Leader* (Lexington: The University Press of Kentucky, 2008), p. 147.

[16]Dănuț Mănăstireanu, ed., *People of Faith, People of Justice* (Iași, Romania: Adoramus Publishers, 2010), p. 59.

[17]Henry H. Mitchell, *Black Preaching: The Recovery of a Powerful Art* (Nashville: Abingdon Press, 1990), p. 108.

[18]Jackson, *Becoming King*, p. 180.

[19]Marsh, *Beloved Community*, p. 49.

[20]Jackson, *Becoming King*, p. 1.

[21]Ibid., p. xi.

[22]Ibid., p. 157.

[23]Ibid., p. 7.

[24]Ibid., p. 180.

[25]Marsh, *Beloved Community*, p. 209.

[26]Lewis Baldwin, *Never to Leave Us Alone: The Prayer Life of Martin Luther King Jr.* (Minneapolis: Fortress Press, 2010), p. 1.

[27]Garrow, *Bearing the Cross*, p. 56.

[28]Ibid., p. 58.

[29]Richard Lischer, *The Preacher King: Martin Luther King Jr. and the Word that Moved America* (New York: Oxford University Press, 1995), p. 89.

[30]Mitchell, *Black Preaching*, p. 130.

[31]Jackson, *Becoming King*, p. xx.

[32]Lischer, *The Preacher King*, p. 177.

[33]Baldwin, *Never to Leave Us Alone*, p. 44.

[34]Charles Marsh, *God's Long Summer: Stories of Faith and Civil Rights* (Princeton, N.J.: Princeton University Press, 1997), p. 6.

[35]Gary Burge, interview with author, August 9, 2011. All quotations in this section are from this interview.

[36]Gary Burge, *Jesus and the Land: The New Testament Challenge to "Holy Land" Theology* (Grand Rapids: Baker Academic, 2010); and Burge, *Whose Land?*

Whose Promise? What Christians Are Not Being Told about Israel and the Palestinians (Cleveland, Ohio: Pilgrim Press, 2004).

[37]Marsh, *Beloved Community*, p. 208.

[38]Richard J. Foster, *Streams of Living Water: Celebrating the Great Traditions of Christian Faith* (San Francisco: HarperCollins, 1998), p. 174.

[39]Jackson, *Becoming King*, p. 168.

[40]Curtiss Paul DeYoung, *Coming Together in the 21st Century: The Bible's Message in an Age of Diversity* (Valley Forge, Penn.: Judson Press, 2009).

[41]Shane Claiborne, *The Irresistible Revolution: Living as an Ordinary Radical* (Grand Rapids: Zondervan, 2006); Scott Bessenecker, *The New Friars: The Emerging Movement Serving the World's Poor* (Downers Grove, Ill.: InterVarsity Press, 2006).

[42]Parker Palmer, *Let Your Life Speak: Listening for the Voice of Vocation* (San Francisco: Jossey-Bass, 1999).

[43]Daniel Taylor, *Tell Me a Story: The Life-Shaping Power of Our Stories* (St. Paul: Bog Walk Press, 2001), p. vii.

Chapter 5
FAIRUZ: *From Worship to Freedom*

[1]Lyrics of *"Esta-niri"* or "Be Enlightened," Tasheba of the Coptic Orthodox Church, accessed December 10, 2011, <http://tasbeha.org/hymn_library/view/1702>.

[2]Quintard Taylor, "Bloody Sunday, Selma, Alabama (March 7, 1965)," *BlackPast.org*, accessed December 10, 2011, <http://www.blackpast.org/?q=aah/bloody-sunday-selma-alabama-march-7-1965>.

[3]Troy Jackson, *Becoming King: Martin Luther King Jr. and the Making of a National Leader* (Lexington: The University Press of Kentucky, 2008), p. 184.

[4]Mary Elizabeth King, "From Selma to Syria: The Power of Nonviolent Resistance," *Sojo Blog*, July 26, 2011, <http://blog.sojo.net/2011/07/26/from-selma-to-syria-the-power-of-song-in-nonviolent-resistance/>.

[5]Ibid.

[6]David J. Garrow, *Bearing the Cross: Martin Luther King Jr. and the Southern Christian Leadership Conference* (New York: HarperCollins, 1986), p. 183.

[7]Martin Luther King Jr., quoted in James M. Washington, ed., *I Have a Dream: Writings and Speeches that Changed the World* (San Francisco: HarperCollins, 1992), p. 197.

[8]Henry H. Mitchell, *Black Preaching: The Recovery of a Powerful Art* (Nashville: Abingdon Press, 1990), p. 16.

[9]"A Legend: Biography," Fairuz Online, accessed December 10, 2011, <http://fairuzonline.com/alegend.htm>.

[10]Ibid.

[11]Ibid.

[12]Ibid.

[13]Michael Frishkopf, *Music and Media in the Arab World* (New York: American University in Cairo Press, 2010), p. 98.

[14]"A Legend: Biography."

[15]Frishkopf, *Music and Media in the Arab World*, p. 98.

[16]Ibid.

[17]Ibid.

[18]"A Legend: Biography."

[19]Ibid.

[20]Ibid. The Melkites are another Eastern sect with ecclesiastical status among the Eastern Rite Catholic Patriarchate of Antioch.

[21]Ibid.

[22]"The Latest: Good Friday, April 2005," Fairuz Online, accessed December 10, 2011, <http://www.fairuzonline.com/tl_goodfriday.htm>.

[23]"The Latest: Good Friday, April 2005."

[24]Ibid.

[25]Lyrics of *"Almasiho Qam"* or "Christ Has Risen," Tasheba of the Coptic Orthodox Church, accessed December 10, 2011, <http://tasbeha.org/hymn_library/view/1703>.

[26]Ibid.

[27]"*Esta-niri*" or "Be Enlightened," Tasheba of the Coptic Orthodox Church.

[28]Lyrics of *"Ya Zahrat al Madayn"* or "Flower of the Cities" on Lyrics Translate, accessed December 10, 2011, <http://lyricstranslate.com/en/node/77817>.

[29]Mary Elizabeth King, "From Selma to Syria."

[30]Ibid.

[31]Ibid.

[32]"John Newton: Reformed Slave Trader," *Christian History*, August 8, 2008, <http://www.christianitytoday.com/ch/131christians/pastorsandpreachers/newton.html?start=1>.

[33]Richard J. Foster, *Streams of Living Water: Celebrating the Great Traditions of Christian Faith* (San Francisco: HarperCollins, 1998), p. 150.

[34]James F. White, *Introduction to Christian Worship* (Nashville: Abingdon Press, 2000), p. 31.

[35]Quoted in ibid., p. 23.

[36]Ibid., p. 23.

[37]Ibid., p. 22.

[38]Ibid., p. 23.

[39]Ibid., p. 18.

[40]Ibid., p. 26.

[41]Ibid., p. 19.

[42]Ibid., p. 19.

[43]Ibid., p. 19. "Bath" refers to the observation of the sacrament of baptism.

[44]Ibid., p. 176.

[45]Ibid., p. 192.

[46]Ibid., p. 191.

[47]Wenche Miriam, email message to author, November 29, 2011. All quotations in this section are from this email correspondence.

[48]Rory Noland, The Heart of the Artist: A Character-Building Guide for You and Your Ministry Team (Grand Rapids: Zondervan, 1999), p. 314.

[49]Ibid., p. 20.

[50]Ibid., p. 17.

[51]"God of Justice (We Must Go)" lyrics by Tim Hughes, Higher Praise, accessed April 29, 2012, <http://www.higherpraise.com/lyrics/awesome/awesome4368.html>.

[52]Bono, Keynote address at the 54th National Prayer Breakfast, February 2, 2006, American Rhetoric Online Speech Bank, <http://www.american rhetoric.com/speeches/bononationalprayerbreakfast.htm>.

[53]Visit EthnoGraphic Media's website at <www.egmfilms.org>.

[54]Dietrich Bonhoeffer, Life Together: A Discussion of Christian Fellowship, trans. John W. Doberstein (New York: Harper & Row Publishers, 1954), p. 58.

[55]Nancy Beach, An Hour on Sunday: Creating Moments of Transformation and Wonder (Grand Rapids: Zondervan, 2004).

Chapter 6
DESMOND TUTU: *From Sabbath to Reconciliation*

[1]Desmond Tutu, God Has a Dream: A Vision of Hope for Our Time (New York: Doubleday Religion, 2004), p. 128.

[2]John H. Walton, The Lost World of Genesis One: Ancient Cosmology and the Origins Debate (Downers Grove, Ill.: InterVarsity Press, 2009), p. 78.

[3]Laurel Baldwin-Ragaven, Leslie London and Jeanelle de Gruchy, Ambulances of the Wrong Colour: Health Professionals, Human Rights and Ethics in South Africa (Cape Town, S.A.: University of Cape Town Press, 1999), p. 18.

[4]Dănuţ Mănăstireanu, ed., People of Faith, People of Justice (Iaşi, Romania: Adoramus Publishers, 2010), p. 66.

[5]Ibid., p. 66.

[6]Ibid., p. 66.

[7]Tutu, God Has a Dream, p. 6.

[8]Ibid., pp. 6-7.

[9]Ibid., pp. 6-7.

[10]Mănăstireanu, People of Faith, p. 66.

[11]Tutu, God Has a Dream, p. 10.

[12]Ibid., p. 10.

[13]Ibid., p. 53.

[14]Ibid., p. 54.

[15]Ibid., p. 57.

[16]Ibid., p. 57.

[17]Ibid., p. 57.

[18]Ibid., p. 17.

[19]Ibid., pp. 1-2.

[20]Ibid., p. 2.

[21]Ibid., pp. 26.

[22]Ibid.

[23]Ibid., p. 49.

[24]Ibid., p. 49.

[25]Mae Elise Cannon, *Social Justice Handbook: Small Steps for a Better World* (Downers Grove, Ill.: InterVarsity Press, 2009), p. 25.

[26]This entire section is revised from Cannon, *Social Justice Handbook,* pp. 27-28.

[27]Mănăstireanu, *People of Faith,* p. 66.

[28]Desmond Tutu and Mpho Tutu, *Made for Goodness: And Why This Makes All the Difference* (New York: HarperOne, 2010), p. 35.

[29]Tutu, *God Has a Dream,* pp. 49-50.

[30]Ibid., p. 128.

[31]Ibid.

[32]Daniel Hill, interview with author, September 13, 2011. All quotations in this section, unless otherwise indicated, are from this interview.

[33]River City Community Church website, accessed April 29, 2012, <http://www.churchwebsites.com/rivercity/index.cfm?page=6>.

[34]Daniel Hill, "Claiming Your Vocational Call," (sermon, River City Community Church, Chicago, Ill., May 29, 2005).

[35]Ibid.

[36]John Ortberg, *The Life You've Always Wanted* (Grand Rapids: Zondervan, 1997), p. 203.

[37]Jenny Trees, a student in Helen Cepero's spiritual formation class at North Park, shared class notes in an email message to the author, November 22, 2011.

[38]James Bryan Smith, *The Good and Beautiful God: Falling in Love with the God Jesus Knows* (Downers Grove, Ill.: InterVarsity Press, 2009), p. 34.

[39]Ibid.

[40]Class notes, Jenny Trees's email message to author, November 22, 2011.

[41]Smith, *Good and Beautiful God,* p. 34.

[42]Tutu and Tutu, *Made for Goodness,* p. 12.

[43]"Workplaces for Sabbaticals," *Your Sabbatical,* accessed January 8, 2012, <http://yoursabbatical.com/learn/workplaces-for-sabbaticals/>.

[44]David J. Garrow, *Bearing the Cross: Martin Luther King Jr. and the Southern Christian Leadership Conference* (New York: HarperCollins Publishers, 1986), p. 125.

Chapter 7
OSCAR ROMERO: *From Submission to Martyrdom*

[1]*Dictionary.com*, s.v. "submit," accessed December 9, 2011, <http://dictionary.reference.com/browse/submit>.

[2]Dănuţ Mănăstireanu, ed., *People of Faith, People of Justice* (Iaşi, Romania: Adoramus Publishers, 2010), p. 60.

[3]Ibid., p. 60.

[4]Scott Wright, *Oscar Romero and the Communion of Saints: A Biography* (Maryknoll, N.Y.: Orbis Books, 2009), p. 10.

[5]Mănăstireanu, *People of Faith*, p. 60.

[6]Wright, *Oscar Romero*, p. 13.

[7]Ibid., p. 16.

[8]Ibid., pp. 24, 27.

[9]Ibid., p. 17.

[10]James R. Brockman, *Romero: A Life* (Maryknoll, N.Y.: Orbis Books, 2005), p. 60.

[11]Mănăstireanu, *People of Faith*, p. 60.

[12]Wright, *Oscar Romero*, p. 22.

[13]Mănăstireanu, *People of Faith*, p. 60.

[14]Wright, *Oscar Romero*, p. 23.

[15]Ibid., p. 33.

[16]Ibid., p. 35.

[17]Brockman, *Romero*, p. 7.

[18]Wright, *Oscar Romero*, p. 41.

[19]Ibid., p. 41.

[20]Brockman, *Romero*, p. 9.

[21]Wright, *Oscar Romero*, p. 39.

[22]Brockman, *Romero*, p. 13.

[23]Mănăstireanu, *People of Faith*, p. 61.

[24]Wright, *Oscar Romero*, p. 54.

[25]Ibid., p. 50.

[26]Ibid., p. 44.

[27]Ibid., p. 45.

[28]Ibid., p. 57.

[29]Oscar Romero, *The Violence of Love*, trans. James R. Brockman, S.J. (Maryknoll, N.Y.: Orbis Books, 2009), p. 153.

[30]Brockman, *Romero*, p. 63.

[31]Romero, *Violence of Love*, p. 180.

[32]Wright, *Oscar Romero*, p. 23.

[33]Romero, *Violence of Love*, p. 187.

[34]Brockman, *Romero*, p. 41.

[35]Ibid., p. 41.

[36]Romero, *Violence of Love*, p. 197.

[37]Brockman, *Romero,* p. 194.
[38]Romero, *Violence of Love,* p. xiii.
[39]Ibid., p. 161.
[40]Ibid., p. 192.
[41]Matt Woodley, *Gospel of Matthew: God with Us* (Downers Grove, Ill.: Inter-Varsity Press, 2011), p. 68.
[42]Romero, *Violence of Love,* p. 117.
[43]Brockman, *Romero,* p. 230.
[44]Romero, *Violence of Love,* p. 14.
[45]Ibid., pp. 87-88.
[46]Ibid., pp. 83-84.
[47]Ibid., p. 152.
[48]Brockman, *Romero,* p. 248.
[49]Woodley, *Gospel of Matthew,* p. 68.
[50]Brockman, *Romero,* p. 244.
[51]Woodley, *Gospel of Matthew,* p. 68.
[52]Wright, *Oscar Romero,* p. 135.
[53]Ibid., p. 3.
[54]Ibid., p. 4.
[55]Ibid., p. 4.
[56]Romero, *Violence of Love,* p. xi.
[57]"Alexia Salvatierra," Hunt Alternatives Fund, accessed November 5, 2011, <http://www.huntalternatives.org/pages/7723_alexia_salvatierra.cfm>.
[58]Alexia Salvatierra, interview with author, August 12, 2011. All quotations in this section are from the same interview.
[59]Richard Foster, *Celebration of Discipline: The Path to Spiritual Growth* (New York: HarperSanFrancisco, 1998), p. 117.
[60]Ibid., p. 112.
[61]Dietrich Bonhoeffer, *The Cost of Discipleship* (New York: Simon & Schuster, 1995), p. 289.
[62]John Ortberg, *The Life You've Always Wanted* (Grand Rapids: Zondervan, 1997), pp. 119-31.

Chapter 8
COURAGE, JOY AND CELEBRATION

[1]John Ortberg, *The Life You've Always Wanted* (Grand Rapids: Zondervan, 1997), p. 65.
[2]Desmond Tutu, *God Has a Dream: A Vision of Hope for Our Time* (New York: Doubleday Religion, 2005), p. 88.
[3]Ortberg, *Life You've Always Wanted,* p. 70.
[4]"About the Authors," Princess Zulu website, accessed January 8, 2012, www.princesszulu.com.
[5]Princess Kasune Zulu, *Warrior Princess: Fighting for Life with Courage and*

Hope (Downers Grove, Ill.: InterVarsity Press, 2009).

[6]John Ortberg, *The Life You've Always Wanted* (Grand Rapids: Zondervan, 1997), p. 71.

[7]Ibid., p. 73.

[8]Dietrich Bonhoeffer, *Life Together: A Discussion of Christian Fellowship,* trans. John W. Doberstein (New York: Harper & Row Publishers, 1954), p. 68.

[9]Ortberg, *Life You've Always Wanted,* p. 75.

[10]Efrem Smith, interview with author, September 13, 2011. All quotations in this section, unless otherwise noted, are from this interview.

[11]Mother Teresa, *Love: The Words and Inspiration of Mother Teresa* (Boulder, Colo.: Blue Mountain Press) p. 3.

[12]Desmond Tutu and Mpho Tutu, *Made for Goodness: And Why This Makes All the Difference* (New York: HarperOne, 2010), p. 175.

[13]Ibid., p. 49.

[14]Scott Wright, *Oscar Romero and the Communion of Saints* (Maryknoll, N.Y.: Orbis Books, 2009), p. 149.

[15]Desmond Tutu, *God Has a Dream: A Vision of Hope for Our Time* (New York: Doubleday Religion, 2005), pp. 97-98.

[16]Mother Teresa, *Love,* 4.